The Threat Landscape: Navigating Cyber Threat Hunting

Sergey Sokolovea

Sergey Sokolovea is a seasoned cybersecurity expert with over a decade of experience in threat intelligence, cyber threat hunting, and digital forensics. Known for his analytical precision and innovative approach to tackling modern cyber threats, Sergey has built a career focused on helping organizations protect their assets from ever-evolving adversaries. His journey in cybersecurity began with a curiosity for understanding the motivations and methods behind cyberattacks, and it quickly developed into a passionate pursuit of proactive, hands-on defense strategies.

With a background in computer science and extensive hands-on experience in corporate and governmental cybersecurity initiatives, Sergey has led multiple threat hunting teams, designed threat detection frameworks, and developed comprehensive training programs for aspiring threat hunters. His unique insights into the psychology of attackers, combined with his in-depth technical knowledge, enable him to communicate complex cybersecurity concepts in an engaging, accessible way.

In **The Threat Landscape: Navigating Cyber Threat Hunting**, Sergey brings his expertise to the page, offering readers a practical guide that combines theoretical foundations with actionable strategies. Whether you're a cybersecurity professional looking to refine your threat hunting skills or a newcomer eager to enter the field, Sergey's book serves as both a guide and an inspiration in the constantly shifting world of cyber defense.

In today's hyper-connected world, where digital assets are the lifeblood of businesses, governments, and individuals alike, cybersecurity has become both a strategic priority and a fundamental responsibility. Cyber threats are no longer limited to opportunistic hackers or isolated incidents; they are orchestrated by organized groups, state-sponsored actors, and even artificial intelligence. Attackers continuously evolve, employing sophisticated techniques to bypass traditional defenses and exploit weaknesses in complex digital infrastructures. As these threats become more pervasive and damaging, it is clear that relying solely on passive defenses is insufficient. This is where cyber threat hunting becomes crucial.

The Threat Landscape: Navigating Cyber Threat Hunting is designed as both a practical guide and a comprehensive roadmap for security professionals, IT teams, and newcomers to cybersecurity who want to understand and apply the principles of threat hunting. This book goes beyond the basics of cybersecurity by diving into the strategic, technical, and tactical facets of proactive threat hunting, aiming to empower readers to anticipate, detect, and mitigate threats before they escalate into incidents.

Within these pages, you'll find a structured approach to understanding the modern threat landscape, with an emphasis on real-world application. From foundational principles to advanced techniques, this book covers every aspect of cyber threat hunting, equipping you to understand adversaries, recognize suspicious behaviors, and develop effective hunting strategies. Each chapter explores critical concepts, tools, methodologies, and emerging technologies, providing actionable insights and techniques that can be applied in real time.

Whether you're seeking to build a robust threat hunting program, sharpen your analytical skills, or stay ahead of the latest cyber trends, The Threat Landscape offers valuable knowledge and guidance. Cybersecurity is a journey of continuous learning, adaptation, and vigilance, and with this book, you'll be better prepared to navigate the challenges and uncertainties that define the ever-shifting cyber battlefield.

Welcome to the hunt.

1. Introduction to Cyber Threat Hunting

In an era where cyber threats are increasingly sophisticated and pervasive, the importance of proactive defense strategies has never been clearer. This chapter introduces the concept of cyber threat hunting, a critical discipline within cybersecurity that involves actively searching for indicators of compromise and potential vulnerabilities before they can be exploited by malicious actors. Unlike traditional security measures that react to known threats, threat hunting is a proactive approach that empowers organizations to anticipate and mitigate risks, fostering a more resilient cybersecurity posture. As we explore the fundamentals of threat hunting, we will uncover its significance, the unique mindset required for effective hunting, and the transformative role it plays in safeguarding digital assets against ever-evolving adversaries.

1.1 The Fundamentals of Threat Hunting

In the fast-evolving landscape of cybersecurity, organizations face an increasing number of sophisticated cyber threats that can disrupt operations, compromise sensitive data, and undermine customer trust. Traditional security measures, such as firewalls and antivirus software, often fall short in effectively detecting and responding to these threats, especially those that are advanced and persistent. This is where the practice of threat hunting becomes essential. Threat hunting is a proactive approach to cybersecurity that involves actively searching for signs of malicious activity within an organization's network and systems, rather than waiting for alerts from automated security tools. This section will explore the fundamentals of threat hunting, including its definition, objectives, methodologies, and the mindset required for effective execution.

Defining Threat Hunting

At its core, threat hunting is the process of actively seeking out indicators of compromise (IOCs) and signs of malicious activity that may have evaded traditional security defenses. Unlike reactive security measures that respond to alerts generated by security information and event management (SIEM) systems or intrusion detection systems (IDS), threat hunting is a proactive and iterative process. It involves the use of hypotheses, intelligence, and investigative techniques to identify potential threats before they can escalate into full-blown incidents.

Threat hunting is not a one-time event but rather a continuous practice that involves monitoring, analysis, and improvement. By adopting this proactive approach, organizations can enhance their detection capabilities, reduce dwell time (the period an attacker remains undetected within a network), and minimize the potential impact of cyber incidents.

Objectives of Threat Hunting

The primary objectives of threat hunting can be summarized as follows:

Early Detection of Threats: One of the main goals of threat hunting is to identify potential threats at an early stage, before they can cause significant harm. By actively searching for indicators of compromise, threat hunters can uncover malicious activity that may have bypassed automated defenses.

Understanding Adversaries: Threat hunting provides valuable insights into the tactics, techniques, and procedures (TTPs) employed by adversaries. By studying their behaviors and patterns, organizations can better prepare for future attacks and enhance their overall security posture.

Improving Incident Response: The findings from threat hunting efforts can inform and improve incident response plans. By understanding the methods used by attackers, organizations can develop more effective response strategies, reducing the time it takes to contain and remediate incidents.

Enhancing Security Posture: Regular threat hunting activities contribute to a culture of continuous improvement in an organization's security posture. By identifying vulnerabilities and weaknesses, organizations can implement necessary changes to strengthen their defenses and reduce the likelihood of successful attacks.

Methodologies of Threat Hunting

Threat hunting methodologies vary, but they typically follow a structured approach that involves several key steps:

Hypothesis Development: The threat hunting process often begins with the formulation of hypotheses based on threat intelligence, historical data, or observed anomalies. For example, a hypothesis might involve the possibility of credential misuse or lateral movement within the network. Developing a clear hypothesis provides a focused direction for the hunt.

Data Collection: Once a hypothesis is established, threat hunters gather relevant data from various sources, such as logs from servers, network traffic, endpoint activity, and threat intelligence feeds. This data is crucial for identifying potential indicators of compromise and understanding the context of the investigation.

Data Analysis: Threat hunters analyze the collected data to look for patterns or anomalies that support or refute their hypotheses. This may involve the use of data analysis techniques, including statistical analysis, behavioral analysis, and machine learning algorithms to identify suspicious activities.

Investigation: If the analysis reveals potential threats or indicators of compromise, threat hunters will conduct further investigations to determine the scope and impact of the detected activity. This phase may involve deep dives into specific systems, interviewing personnel, or utilizing forensic tools to gather additional evidence.

Mitigation and Reporting: After completing the investigation, threat hunters will take appropriate action to mitigate any identified threats, which may include isolating affected systems, applying patches, or enhancing security controls. Furthermore, documenting the findings and sharing insights with relevant stakeholders is essential for improving future threat hunting efforts and incident response.

The Threat Hunter's Mindset

Successful threat hunting requires a specific mindset characterized by curiosity, analytical thinking, and a proactive approach to problem-solving. Threat hunters should possess the following attributes:

Curiosity and Skepticism: A natural curiosity to explore and investigate anomalies is vital. Threat hunters must approach data with a healthy dose of skepticism, always questioning what they observe and looking for hidden patterns or behaviors that may indicate malicious activity.

Analytical Skills: Strong analytical skills are essential for dissecting complex data sets, recognizing patterns, and drawing meaningful conclusions. Threat hunters should be comfortable using various analytical tools and techniques to identify indicators of compromise.

Technical Proficiency: Familiarity with cybersecurity tools, systems, and methodologies is critical. Threat hunters should have a solid understanding of networking, operating systems, and security technologies, enabling them to effectively navigate and analyze the environments they are hunting in.

Collaboration and Communication: Effective threat hunting often involves collaboration with other teams, such as incident response, IT operations, and threat intelligence. Strong communication skills are essential for sharing findings and coordinating efforts to address identified threats.

Continuous Learning: The cybersecurity landscape is constantly changing, with new threats and tactics emerging regularly. A commitment to continuous learning and professional development is crucial for staying ahead of adversaries and adapting threat hunting methodologies accordingly.

In summary, threat hunting is an essential practice in modern cybersecurity that empowers organizations to take a proactive stance against cyber threats. By actively seeking out indicators of compromise and understanding the behaviors of adversaries, threat hunters can enhance detection capabilities, improve incident response efforts, and strengthen overall security posture. Through structured methodologies and the right mindset, organizations can cultivate a culture of vigilance and resilience, ensuring they are better prepared to defend against the ever-evolving threat landscape. As the cyber threat landscape continues to grow in complexity and sophistication, the importance of effective threat hunting cannot be overstated. Organizations that invest in this proactive approach will not only protect their digital assets more effectively but will also gain valuable insights into the tactics used by cyber adversaries, paving the way for a more secure future.

1.2 The Proactive Approach: Why Threat Hunting Matters

In the face of increasingly sophisticated cyber threats, a proactive approach to cybersecurity has become essential. Unlike traditional, reactive security measures that rely on alarms and alerts generated after an attack has already begun, threat hunting focuses on identifying and neutralizing threats before they can cause harm. This shift from a reactive to a proactive security mindset is crucial for modern organizations looking to reduce both the frequency and impact of cyber incidents. Threat hunting not only empowers organizations to anticipate potential attacks but also fosters a deeper understanding of an organization's security weaknesses and the tactics used by adversaries. This section explores the reasons why threat hunting matters, emphasizing its role in minimizing risks, reducing response times, and strengthening an organization's overall resilience.

Understanding the Reactive Limitations

Traditional cybersecurity measures, such as firewalls, antivirus software, and intrusion detection systems (IDS), are essential components of any security strategy. However, these tools are inherently reactive, often focusing on known threats and generating alerts based on pre-established rules or signature-based detections. While these tools play a critical role, they are not always effective at identifying sophisticated attacks that exploit unknown vulnerabilities, employ custom malware, or use techniques that evade detection. Reactive security systems are also vulnerable to false negatives, where certain threats remain undetected due to limited knowledge of the attack methods used by advanced adversaries.

The problem with a purely reactive approach is that it often allows attackers to remain within a network undetected for extended periods—a phenomenon known as "dwell time." During this time, attackers can explore networks, steal sensitive data, and expand their foothold within an organization. Threat hunting addresses this gap by proactively searching for potential threats, even those that may not trigger traditional security alerts.

Anticipating and Reducing Dwell Time

Reducing dwell time is one of the most critical goals of threat hunting. The longer an attacker remains undetected within a network, the greater the potential for damage. Extended dwell time can result in data breaches, intellectual property theft, ransomware deployment, and more. Threat hunting helps mitigate these risks by identifying and addressing threats early in the attack cycle.

By actively searching for signs of compromise, such as unusual network behavior, login anomalies, or suspicious processes running on endpoints, threat hunters can disrupt attacks before they escalate. Reducing dwell time not only limits the potential harm caused by cyber adversaries but also demonstrates an organization's commitment to maintaining a proactive and resilient security posture.

Enhancing Detection Capabilities and Reducing Response Times

One of the most significant benefits of threat hunting is its ability to enhance an organization's detection capabilities. Because threat hunting focuses on finding signs of malicious activity that have evaded traditional defenses, it allows organizations to identify new attack vectors and TTPs (tactics, techniques, and procedures) employed by cyber adversaries. This deeper level of detection can reveal blind spots in existing security controls, allowing security teams to enhance their monitoring systems and develop new detection rules or alerts.

Additionally, by identifying threats early in the attack lifecycle, threat hunting helps organizations respond faster and more effectively to potential incidents. Faster response times reduce the duration and impact of incidents, limiting damage to data, systems, and overall business operations. Threat hunting also strengthens collaboration between the hunting team and incident response teams, leading to more efficient and coordinated responses to detected threats.

Building a Resilient Security Posture

Resilience in cybersecurity refers to an organization's ability to withstand and quickly recover from cyber incidents. Threat hunting plays a critical role in building this resilience by continuously improving detection capabilities and preparing for emerging threats. By regularly engaging in threat hunting activities, organizations can identify and address vulnerabilities, whether they stem from unpatched software, misconfigured systems, or gaps in monitoring.

Furthermore, threat hunting fosters a culture of continuous learning and improvement within the security team. As threat hunters encounter new adversaries and techniques, they document their findings, which can be used to update security protocols and train other team members. This ongoing process of discovery, documentation, and training helps organizations adapt to the rapidly changing threat landscape, ensuring they remain resilient against both current and future threats.

Understanding the Adversary's Mindset

Effective threat hunting requires security teams to think like adversaries, anticipating how attackers might attempt to infiltrate, navigate, and exploit an organization's systems. This adversarial mindset is crucial in identifying potential weaknesses and understanding the motives and strategies of different threat actors, whether they are financially motivated cybercriminals, politically motivated hacktivists, or state-sponsored groups. By examining attacks from an adversary's perspective, threat hunters can create hypotheses based on possible attack vectors, test the effectiveness of their defenses, and identify areas where security measures may fall short.

In addition, by understanding the specific tactics and techniques used by threat actors, organizations can improve their defenses in targeted ways. For example, if threat hunters identify a tendency for attackers to use certain remote access tools or lateral movement techniques, they can implement additional monitoring and detection capabilities to prevent these methods from succeeding in the future.

Aligning with Business Objectives

A proactive approach to cybersecurity not only minimizes risks but also aligns with broader business objectives. Cyber incidents can disrupt operations, damage an organization's reputation, and result in significant financial costs due to downtime, legal liabilities, and regulatory fines. By investing in threat hunting, organizations demonstrate their commitment to protecting customer data, safeguarding proprietary information, and ensuring operational continuity.

Moreover, threat hunting helps organizations comply with regulatory requirements and industry standards, many of which emphasize the importance of proactive measures to prevent data breaches and protect sensitive information. Implementing a threat hunting program signals to regulators, partners, and customers that the organization is committed to maintaining robust security practices, which can enhance trust and reduce the likelihood of compliance issues.

In an era where cyber threats continue to grow in complexity and scale, threat hunting represents a critical shift from reactive to proactive security. By actively seeking out potential threats, organizations can reduce dwell time, improve detection capabilities, and build a resilient security posture that is prepared for both current and future threats. Threat hunting empowers organizations to think like adversaries, anticipate emerging risks, and make informed improvements to their defenses, ultimately contributing to safer and more reliable digital environments. By embracing a proactive approach, organizations not only protect their assets more effectively but also gain a strategic advantage in the ongoing battle against cyber adversaries.

1.3 The Threat Hunter's Mindset

The success of threat hunting hinges not only on skill and tools but also on a distinctive mindset that combines curiosity, persistence, and an adversarial perspective. Effective threat hunters don't just react to alerts or follow a checklist—they actively question assumptions, dig into anomalies, and think like an attacker. This unique mindset drives them to uncover hidden threats, detect sophisticated attacks, and enhance the organization's overall cybersecurity posture. Developing the threat hunter's mindset is as crucial as mastering technical skills because it enables security professionals to go beyond reactive measures and proactively address threats that evade traditional detection. In this section, we will delve into the core qualities that shape the mindset of a successful threat hunter, focusing on curiosity, persistence, skepticism, creativity, and adaptability.

Curiosity: The Drive to Dig Deeper

Curiosity is the fuel that propels threat hunters to go beyond surface-level observations and explore the unknown. Effective threat hunters are naturally inclined to ask "why" and "how," allowing them to uncover unusual patterns, understand complex attack vectors, and dig into anomalies that might otherwise go unnoticed. Rather than accepting data at face value, curious threat hunters dive deeper, investigating the root causes of suspicious behavior.

For instance, when encountering an unfamiliar process or network connection, a curious threat hunter won't simply note it as "suspicious" or "benign." They will investigate further, asking questions like, "What triggered this connection?" or "Has this process been observed before?" By being relentlessly curious, threat hunters can identify potential threats that evade typical detection and gain insights into attacker behaviors and techniques.

Persistence: Staying the Course Amid Complexity

Cyber threats are often complex, involving multiple stages and varied tactics that make detection challenging. Persistence is a key trait of a successful threat hunter, allowing them to stay focused, dig through large datasets, and follow leads that may initially appear trivial but could uncover significant threats. This tenacity is especially important when threat hunters face challenges such as incomplete data, obscure attack vectors, or advanced evasion techniques.

Persistence also involves a commitment to iterative hunting. Threat hunters know that not every lead will yield a clear answer or immediate results; sometimes, they may need to revisit findings, refine hypotheses, and repeatedly test their assumptions. This dedication to following through is essential for uncovering sophisticated attacks that require multiple passes and deep analysis to understand.

Healthy Skepticism: Questioning Assumptions and Patterns

Threat hunters approach data with a healthy skepticism, questioning both the information they're presented with and the systems that generate it. This skepticism prevents them from relying solely on automated alerts or high-confidence data points, which can sometimes produce false positives or mask deeper issues. Skeptical threat hunters scrutinize each data source, questioning anomalies, seeking inconsistencies, and validating assumptions before reaching a conclusion.

This skepticism also applies to interpreting historical patterns or existing baselines. Skilled threat hunters understand that while baselines are useful, they are not foolproof, as attackers can often disguise their actions within normal-seeming activities. By questioning assumptions, threat hunters avoid complacency, ensuring they remain alert to subtle deviations that could indicate a potential threat.

Adversarial Thinking: Understanding the Attacker's Mindset

Thinking like an adversary is one of the most essential aspects of the threat hunter's mindset. By putting themselves in the attacker's shoes, threat hunters can anticipate likely attack paths, techniques, and targets, enabling them to proactively search for indicators of compromise that might otherwise go overlooked. Adversarial thinking involves asking questions like, "If I were the attacker, where would I hide?" or "How would I navigate through this network undetected?"

This mindset helps threat hunters understand the motivations and methods behind various threat actors, from financially motivated cybercriminals to state-sponsored groups. For instance, a financially motivated attacker might prioritize stealing customer data or deploying ransomware, while an espionage-focused group might seek long-term access to sensitive information. By understanding these motives, threat hunters can tailor their searches to potential attack vectors and behaviors relevant to specific threats, making their investigations more targeted and effective.

Creativity: Finding Innovative Solutions to Complex Problems

Cyber adversaries are constantly developing new tactics to evade detection, requiring threat hunters to be equally innovative in their approach to identifying and addressing threats. Creativity allows threat hunters to think outside conventional methods and apply novel techniques when traditional approaches fall short. Whether it's creating custom scripts, using advanced analytics, or exploring unique data sources, creativity enables threat hunters to solve problems that require more than standard tools and techniques.

For example, when looking for lateral movement within a network, a creative threat hunter might use behavioral analytics to identify anomalies that suggest credential misuse or unauthorized access patterns rather than relying on simple log analysis. This inventive approach can reveal threats that evade typical detection methods, adding an extra layer of sophistication to the hunting process.

Adaptability: Staying Agile in an Evolving Threat Landscape

The cyber threat landscape is continuously evolving, with attackers developing new techniques and exploiting emerging vulnerabilities. Adaptability is crucial for threat hunters to stay effective in the face of these changes, as it allows them to quickly learn and apply new skills, technologies, and methodologies. Threat hunters with this quality are comfortable with change and can rapidly pivot their focus when they encounter unexpected or novel threats.

Adaptability also involves a commitment to continuous learning. As cyber threats and security technologies evolve, threat hunters must stay updated on the latest tools, methodologies, and attack patterns. Regularly attending training, following industry trends, and engaging with the broader cybersecurity community are all ways that adaptable threat hunters keep their skills sharp and relevant.

The Value of Continuous Improvement

The threat hunter's mindset is rooted in a philosophy of continuous improvement. Every hunt provides valuable lessons, whether it reveals an actual threat, a potential vulnerability, or simply an opportunity to enhance an existing detection method. Skilled threat hunters document their findings and share insights with their teams, creating a feedback loop that enhances future hunts. This ongoing refinement process not only builds individual expertise but also strengthens the organization's security posture as a whole.

Continuous improvement also applies to the development of hypotheses and hunting techniques. For instance, if a hypothesis about lateral movement doesn't yield any findings, the threat hunter may re-evaluate their assumptions, considering alternative attack paths or potential blind spots. This iterative approach ensures that threat hunters don't rely on stale hypotheses but instead constantly refine their strategies in response to the latest intelligence and trends.

The threat hunter's mindset is a blend of curiosity, persistence, skepticism, creativity, and adaptability—qualities that go beyond technical skills to empower security professionals in the proactive fight against cyber threats. This mindset equips threat hunters to look beyond the obvious, think like attackers, and constantly refine their approach to finding hidden threats. By embracing this proactive and investigative mentality, organizations can cultivate a security culture that is not only resilient to today's cyber challenges but also agile enough to adapt to the evolving threat landscape.

2. Understanding the Modern Threat Landscape

The cyber landscape is an intricate and dynamic environment where threats are continually evolving, driven by technological advancements and the increasing sophistication of malicious actors. In this chapter, we will delve into the various types of cyber threats that organizations face today, including malware, ransomware, advanced persistent threats (APTs), and insider threats. We will explore the motivations and tactics of different adversaries—ranging from individual hackers to organized cybercriminal groups and state-sponsored actors—each with their unique objectives and methods. Additionally, we will examine the latest trends in cybercrime and how they influence the tactics, techniques, and procedures (TTPs) employed by attackers. By gaining a comprehensive understanding of the modern threat landscape, you will be better equipped to identify, anticipate, and respond to the diverse range of threats that pose risks to your organization's security.

2.1 Key Threat Types and Their Impact

In today's digital ecosystem, cyber threats come in various forms, each with unique tactics, techniques, and potential impacts on organizations. Understanding the primary types of cyber threats—and the specific risks each poses—provides a foundational awareness that is crucial for effective threat hunting. By identifying these key threat types, organizations can tailor their defenses and threat hunting strategies to proactively detect and counteract them. In this section, we'll explore some of the most prevalent threat types, including malware, phishing, ransomware, insider threats, and advanced persistent threats (APTs), and examine their impact on organizations.

1. Malware: The Versatile Attacker

Malware, short for "malicious software," is one of the most common forms of cyber threat and encompasses various types of harmful software, such as viruses, worms, trojans, and spyware. Each type of malware has distinct characteristics and attack methods, but all aim to compromise systems and gain unauthorized access to information.

Impact: Malware can cause a range of damage, from minor disruptions to catastrophic data breaches. For instance, spyware can steal sensitive information, while ransomware encrypts files and demands a ransom payment to restore access. The financial cost of malware-related breaches is often substantial, including expenses for remediation, lost productivity, and potential reputational damage.

Example in Threat Hunting: Malware detection often involves analyzing anomalous file behaviors, unusual access patterns, or suspicious processes. Threat hunters focus on identifying signs of malware in both network traffic and endpoint activity, which helps in early detection and mitigation.

2. Phishing: Social Engineering at Scale

Phishing attacks exploit human psychology to manipulate individuals into divulging confidential information, such as login credentials, financial information, or other sensitive data. Attackers typically impersonate legitimate entities to gain the victim's trust, using emails, messages, or websites that appear authentic.

Impact: Phishing can result in unauthorized access to systems, data breaches, and financial fraud. Phishing attacks are also commonly used to deliver malware, leading to secondary attacks. The effects of phishing can be wide-ranging, from minor account compromises to major data breaches that impact millions of individuals.

Example in Threat Hunting: Threat hunters monitor for indicators like suspicious login attempts, unusual access locations, or large volumes of outbound emails that could suggest a phishing compromise. Additionally, they may investigate patterns in email traffic to identify potential spear-phishing campaigns targeting specific employees.

3. Ransomware: Extortion at Scale

Ransomware is a type of malware that encrypts an organization's data, making it inaccessible until a ransom is paid. Recent ransomware attacks have become more sophisticated, often involving "double extortion," where attackers not only encrypt the data but also threaten to release it publicly if the ransom is not paid.

Impact: Ransomware has significant operational and financial repercussions. It can bring business operations to a halt, and if critical systems are compromised, the financial and reputational costs can be severe. Industries like healthcare and finance are frequent targets due to the sensitivity of their data and the urgency of their operations.

Example in Threat Hunting: Detecting ransomware typically involves identifying telltale signs like unusual file encryption, large volumes of files being modified in quick succession, or communication with known malicious IP addresses associated with ransomware. Threat hunters look for these patterns in endpoint and network data to catch ransomware early in the attack cycle.

4. Insider Threats: The Enemy Within

Insider threats originate from within the organization and can be one of the most difficult threats to detect. Insiders may have legitimate access to systems and data, which makes identifying malicious behavior challenging. These threats can be intentional (such as a disgruntled employee stealing data) or unintentional (such as an employee accidentally exposing sensitive information).

Impact: Insider threats can lead to data leaks, intellectual property theft, financial loss, and damage to an organization's reputation. Because insiders already have access to systems, the financial and reputational damage from these threats can be extensive.

Example in Threat Hunting: Threat hunters look for anomalies in user behavior that could indicate malicious intent, such as unusual data transfers, access to sensitive files without a clear need, or login attempts outside normal working hours. User behavior analytics (UBA) and anomaly detection are crucial in identifying potential insider threats.

5. Advanced Persistent Threats (APTs): Stealthy and Strategic

Advanced persistent threats (APTs) are highly sophisticated attacks, often orchestrated by well-funded and skilled groups, including state-sponsored actors. APTs involve prolonged and stealthy campaigns that aim to infiltrate, observe, and exfiltrate data from a target organization over an extended period. These attacks are characterized by their persistence, stealth, and adaptability.

Impact: APTs pose a significant risk to organizations, particularly those in critical infrastructure, defense, finance, and government. These attacks can result in the loss of highly sensitive information, espionage, and long-term disruptions. The long-term nature of APTs means that they often go undetected for months, resulting in prolonged access to an organization's network and data.

Example in Threat Hunting: Detecting APTs requires a layered approach, as attackers use multiple tactics to avoid detection. Threat hunters search for patterns of lateral movement, privilege escalation, and use of sophisticated tools that help attackers remain undetected. Monitoring for persistent anomalies in network traffic and file system activity is essential for identifying the presence of an APT.

6. Distributed Denial of Service (DDoS): Overwhelming Attacks

Distributed Denial of Service (DDoS) attacks aim to overwhelm an organization's network or services, rendering them unavailable to legitimate users. Attackers achieve this by flooding the target with massive volumes of requests, often using botnets made up of compromised devices.

Impact: DDoS attacks can disrupt business operations, damage reputations, and incur financial losses due to downtime. While DDoS attacks don't typically involve data breaches, the operational impact can be severe, especially for online services and e-commerce platforms.

Example in Threat Hunting: Detecting DDoS attacks involves monitoring for abnormal spikes in network traffic. Threat hunters analyze traffic patterns and network logs to identify the source of the flood and implement countermeasures to restore service availability.

Each cyber threat type presents unique challenges, making it essential for organizations to understand their specific characteristics and potential impacts. The effectiveness of threat hunting lies in a nuanced approach tailored to detecting these diverse threats. By understanding key threat types like malware, phishing, ransomware, insider threats, APTs, and DDoS attacks, threat hunters can better anticipate adversarial tactics and implement more targeted detection and response strategies. The knowledge of these threat types not only guides proactive threat hunting efforts but also strengthens an organization's ability to defend against both traditional and advanced cyber adversaries.

2.2 Who Are the Adversaries?

Understanding who the adversaries are in the cybersecurity landscape is critical to developing effective threat-hunting strategies and defensive measures. Cyber adversaries are diverse in their motivations, skills, and methods, ranging from independent hackers to state-sponsored groups, each presenting unique challenges and risks to organizations. This chapter explores the main types of adversaries, including cybercriminals, hacktivists, insider threats, nation-state actors, and cyberterrorists, examining their tactics, motivations, and the specific threats they pose.

1. Cybercriminals: Profit-Driven Attackers

Cybercriminals are among the most common adversaries organizations face today. Their primary motivation is financial gain, often through activities such as ransomware attacks, phishing scams, and data theft for resale on the dark web. Cybercriminals range in sophistication, from novice hackers using readily available malware to organized cybercrime syndicates that run sophisticated operations akin to traditional businesses.

Tactics and Techniques: Cybercriminals rely heavily on tactics like phishing, social engineering, and malware distribution to compromise systems and extract valuable information. Ransomware attacks have become a particularly lucrative tool for these adversaries, who use encryption to block access to critical data and demand payments for its release.

Impact on Organizations: Cybercriminals can disrupt business operations, steal sensitive data, and cause significant financial losses through both direct theft and operational downtime. Organizations in any sector can be a target, but cybercriminals often focus on industries with valuable data or critical services, such as finance, healthcare, and e-commerce.

2. Hacktivists: Ideologically Motivated Attackers

Hacktivists are attackers who are driven by social, political, or environmental causes rather than financial gain. These adversaries use hacking as a tool for activism, often aiming to promote a cause, expose perceived injustices, or disrupt the operations of organizations they view as unethical.

Tactics and Techniques: Hacktivists typically target websites, social media platforms, and other public-facing systems. Their attacks often include distributed denial-of-service (DDoS) attacks to bring down websites, defacement of websites to spread messages, and leaks of sensitive data to expose misconduct or corruption.

Impact on Organizations: Hacktivists can cause reputational damage, disrupt services, and lead to data exposure. While the financial losses may be less severe than those caused by cybercriminals, the public and reputational impact of a hacktivist attack can be long-lasting, affecting an organization's trust and credibility with customers.

3. Insider Threats: Internal Risks from Authorized Users

Insider threats arise from within an organization, typically from employees, contractors, or trusted partners with authorized access to systems and data. These adversaries may act out of personal grievances, financial incentives, or by accident, posing risks from both intentional and unintentional actions.

Tactics and Techniques: Insider threats vary in form, from data theft and sabotage to accidental leaks of sensitive information. Malicious insiders may take advantage of their access to download confidential files, install malware, or alter system settings to disrupt operations.

Impact on Organizations: Insider threats are challenging to detect because insiders have legitimate access to systems. The damage can be extensive, including data breaches, intellectual property theft, and operational disruptions. Organizations must be especially vigilant with privileged access and monitor unusual internal activity to mitigate these risks.

4. Nation-State Actors: Sophisticated and Strategic Threats

Nation-state actors represent some of the most advanced and persistent adversaries in cybersecurity. These state-sponsored groups have extensive resources, including funding, training, and sophisticated technology. Their motivations are often political or strategic, with objectives that range from espionage to the disruption of critical infrastructure in target countries.

Tactics and Techniques: Nation-state actors utilize advanced persistent threats (APTs) to infiltrate and remain in target networks for extended periods, gathering intelligence or positioning for future disruptions. They may employ zero-day exploits, custom malware, and stealthy lateral movement techniques to avoid detection. Their attacks are usually highly targeted and meticulously planned, with specific goals aligned with the interests of the sponsoring nation.

Impact on Organizations: The impact of nation-state attacks can be significant, especially for government agencies, critical infrastructure providers, and sectors with valuable intellectual property, such as technology and defense. These attacks can lead to data theft, disruption of essential services, and geopolitical repercussions. Because of their sophistication, nation-state actors often go undetected for long periods, making them difficult to counter without advanced threat-hunting capabilities.

5. Cyberterrorists: Attacks Aimed at Causing Widespread Disruption

Cyberterrorists are groups or individuals who use cyber attacks to instill fear, disrupt societies, or advance political agendas. Unlike hacktivists, who typically target specific organizations for specific causes, cyberterrorists aim for large-scale impact and often target critical infrastructure, such as power grids, transportation systems, and financial institutions.

Tactics and Techniques: Cyberterrorists may use techniques similar to those of other cybercriminals, such as DDoS attacks, malware, and ransomware. However, their ultimate goal is not financial gain but widespread disruption, panic, and societal impact. They may also use coordinated attacks on multiple systems to amplify their effects.

Impact on Organizations: The impact of cyberterrorism can be devastating, particularly when it targets critical infrastructure. These attacks can lead to public safety risks, operational shutdowns, and a loss of public confidence in essential services. Organizations facing cyberterrorist threats must prioritize resilience and preparedness, as these attacks can have far-reaching consequences for society as a whole.

6. Script Kiddies and Novice Hackers: Opportunistic and Low-Skill Attacks

Script kiddies are inexperienced hackers who use pre-made tools, scripts, and exploit kits to carry out attacks. While they may lack advanced skills and a deeper understanding of the systems they target, script kiddies can still pose a risk by exploiting known vulnerabilities and causing disruptions.

Tactics and Techniques: Script kiddies rely on widely available hacking tools and techniques, such as port scanning, password guessing, and exploiting outdated software vulnerabilities. Their attacks are often random and opportunistic, rather than targeted, but they can still cause harm to organizations with weak security practices.

Impact on Organizations: Although less sophisticated, script kiddies can still cause damage, particularly if they exploit overlooked vulnerabilities or poor security hygiene. The impact is typically lower compared to more skilled adversaries, but these attacks serve as a reminder of the importance of maintaining basic cybersecurity practices and updating systems regularly.

The cybersecurity landscape is populated by a wide range of adversaries, each with different motivations, skills, and objectives. From financially driven cybercriminals and ideologically motivated hacktivists to highly skilled nation-state actors and opportunistic script kiddies, understanding these adversaries allows organizations to tailor their threat-hunting strategies accordingly. By anticipating the tactics, techniques, and goals of each type of adversary, organizations can improve their defenses, enhance incident response capabilities, and build a more resilient security posture against today's complex and diverse threat landscape.

2.3 Tactics, Techniques, and Procedures (TTPs)

In cybersecurity, understanding the Tactics, Techniques, and Procedures (TTPs) of adversaries is essential for effective threat detection and response. TTPs offer insight into the specific steps attackers take to achieve their objectives, from initial access to data exfiltration, helping threat hunters anticipate and identify potential threats before they escalate. This section explores the nature of TTPs, their significance in the threat-hunting process, and the ways they enable organizations to stay one step ahead of sophisticated cyber adversaries.

1. Tactics: The Adversary's High-Level Goals

Tactics represent the overarching objectives or goals that adversaries aim to accomplish during a cyber attack. These goals can include actions such as gaining initial access, establishing persistence, moving laterally within a network, and exfiltrating data. Tactics provide a structured view of an adversary's attack progression, breaking down complex operations into identifiable stages.

Examples of Tactics: Key tactics in the cyber kill chain include:

- **Initial Access**: Methods used to infiltrate a target network, such as phishing, exploiting software vulnerabilities, or leveraging stolen credentials.
- **Lateral Movement**: Actions taken to expand access within the network, allowing attackers to reach valuable assets.
- **Exfiltration**: Techniques used to move stolen data out of the target environment, often while avoiding detection.
- **Importance in Threat Hunting**: Understanding an adversary's tactics allows threat hunters to predict potential next steps in an attack and prioritize detection efforts accordingly. For example, if initial access tactics have been identified, threat hunters can focus on detecting subsequent lateral movement or privilege escalation attempts.

2. Techniques: Specific Methods Used to Achieve Tactics

Techniques are the specific methods attackers employ to achieve their tactical goals. They provide a more detailed view of how adversaries approach each phase of an attack, describing the exact ways that attackers execute their strategies. Techniques can include anything from password spraying (as a technique for initial access) to using PowerShell for fileless attacks (a common method for evading detection).

Examples of Techniques:

- **Spear Phishing (for Initial Access):** A targeted form of phishing that tailors messages to specific individuals to increase the likelihood of success.
- **Credential Dumping (for Credential Access):** Using tools to extract credentials from memory or the operating system to gain unauthorized access.
- **Command and Control (C2) Communication (for Maintaining Access):** Establishing a backchannel for remote control over infected devices, often through HTTP/S or other protocols to evade detection.
- **Importance in Threat Hunting**: Techniques give threat hunters a clear, actionable focus for their detection efforts. By knowing specific techniques associated with each tactic, hunters can monitor for key indicators of these techniques, such as unusual PowerShell commands or anomalies in authentication logs. This level of detail is essential for creating robust detection and response strategies tailored to real-world attack behaviors.

3. Procedures: The Unique Execution of Techniques by Specific Threat Actors

Procedures refer to the specific ways in which a given threat actor or group applies known techniques. While tactics and techniques tend to be broad and can apply to various adversaries, procedures are unique to individual groups or actors, often reflecting their resources, skills, and familiarity with the target environment. For instance, two groups might use the same technique of credential dumping, but one might rely on open-source tools while the other uses custom-built malware.

Examples of Procedures:

- **APT29's Use of PowerShell Scripts for Persistence**: While many groups use PowerShell, APT29 might apply it in a specific way, using custom scripts or sequencing steps that distinguish their approach.
- **FIN7's Targeting of POS Systems**: This cybercrime group is known for its focus on point-of-sale systems, leveraging particular malware families to extract payment card information.
- **Custom C2 Servers with Unique Encryption Protocols**: Certain groups will modify the C2 protocol to evade detection, for instance, using obscure ports or encoding commands in ways that evade conventional monitoring systems.
- **Importance in Threat Hunting**: Procedures enable threat hunters to identify specific threat actor patterns and adjust defenses accordingly. By monitoring for known adversary procedures, hunters can detect the presence of a specific actor

earlier, potentially linking an incident to a known group and using that knowledge to anticipate future moves and tailor defenses.

Leveraging TTPs in Threat Hunting

By using TTPs as a framework, threat hunters can detect, analyze, and respond to attacks more effectively. TTPs are essential for developing hunting hypotheses, identifying anomalous behavior, and creating custom detection rules that align with known attack patterns. Here's how each component of TTPs contributes to a more effective threat-hunting strategy:

Building Hypotheses Around Tactics and Techniques: Threat hunters often develop hunting hypotheses by focusing on specific tactics or techniques relevant to their organization's risk profile. For example, if phishing is a common threat, a hypothesis might involve examining email logs for suspicious patterns indicating initial access attempts. TTPs guide hunters to prioritize high-risk areas based on real-world attack patterns.

Using MITRE ATT&CK Framework: A valuable resource in threat hunting, the MITRE ATT&CK framework catalogs tactics and techniques used by known adversaries, mapping them to different stages of the cyber kill chain. By consulting MITRE ATT&CK, threat hunters can identify relevant TTPs for specific types of adversaries, using it as a roadmap for creating and testing detection rules.

Developing Detection Rules for Techniques and Procedures: With detailed knowledge of techniques and procedures, security teams can craft detection rules that look for specific indicators of those techniques. For instance, a detection rule might be set to alert on excessive login attempts across multiple accounts (indicative of password spraying), or on the execution of remote scripts via PowerShell, which is a common technique for lateral movement.

Correlating Events to Identify Attack Progression: By correlating multiple events and behaviors, threat hunters can map the progression of an attack through various tactics, techniques, and even procedures specific to certain threat groups. For example, the presence of suspicious PowerShell commands, followed by unexpected outbound communication, could indicate a progression from initial access to command-and-control activity, helping analysts intervene at an early stage.

The Benefits of TTP-Focused Threat Hunting

Proactive Detection: By focusing on TTPs, threat hunters can proactively search for behaviors that indicate early attack stages, even if there are no immediate signs of compromise.

Enhanced Attribution: Knowing the specific procedures used by threat groups enables better attribution, helping security teams understand which adversaries they may be facing and informing response strategies accordingly.

Improved Incident Response: During incident response, understanding TTPs can expedite the process by highlighting likely next steps, enabling faster containment, remediation, and recovery.

Adaptability to New Threats: As adversaries evolve, so too do their TTPs. By focusing on these foundational elements, threat hunters can adapt more readily to new threats, updating detection rules and hunting methods to keep pace with emerging adversary behaviors.

The study of Tactics, Techniques, and Procedures is a cornerstone of modern threat hunting, providing a structured approach to understanding and anticipating cyber adversaries. TTPs offer a multi-layered insight into how attacks unfold, from broad objectives to the unique methodologies employed by specific groups. By leveraging this knowledge, organizations can proactively seek out and neutralize threats, creating a more resilient and adaptive cybersecurity posture that's responsive to the rapidly evolving threat landscape.

3. Building a Threat Hunting Program

Establishing a successful threat hunting program is essential for organizations seeking to proactively defend against cyber threats and enhance their overall security posture. In this chapter, we will outline the key components necessary for building a robust threat hunting program, including defining its scope, objectives, and methodologies. We will discuss the importance of assembling a skilled and diverse threat hunting team, detailing the roles and responsibilities that contribute to effective collaboration and execution. Additionally, we will explore various frameworks and best practices, such as MITRE ATT&CK, that provide structure and guidance for threat hunting initiatives. By understanding how to effectively build and implement a threat hunting program, organizations can improve their detection capabilities, respond to incidents more efficiently, and create a culture of continuous improvement in their cybersecurity efforts.

3.1 The Essentials of a Threat Hunting Program

Building an effective threat hunting program is critical for any organization looking to proactively identify and mitigate security threats. Unlike traditional security measures, which primarily focus on reactive defenses, a threat hunting program empowers organizations to actively seek out malicious activity, identify vulnerabilities, and continuously improve their defensive posture. This chapter introduces the key components and organizational essentials needed to establish a successful threat hunting program, providing a foundation for both new and mature security teams.

1. Defining Goals and Scope of Threat Hunting

The first step in creating a threat hunting program is clearly defining its objectives and scope. A well-defined purpose ensures that all stakeholders are aligned, resources are appropriately allocated, and the program can effectively mitigate specific risks the organization faces. These goals might include reducing the dwell time of adversaries within the network, increasing visibility into internal activities, or refining the organization's incident response capabilities.

Setting Strategic Objectives: Determining what success looks like for the program involves outlining high-level objectives that align with the organization's broader cybersecurity goals. Objectives may include reducing false positives in detection tools, minimizing the time to detect and respond to threats, and improving overall security posture.

Defining Scope and Boundaries: Threat hunting can cover a vast range of activities, from looking for indicators of compromise in the network to examining user behavior patterns. Clearly defined scope helps teams focus their efforts on critical assets and sensitive data while ensuring they don't exhaust resources on lower-risk areas. Establishing this scope also involves understanding the organization's risk tolerance, which will guide which systems and data should be prioritized.

2. Establishing the Threat Hunting Team

A successful threat hunting program requires a skilled and dedicated team with specialized knowledge in cybersecurity, data analysis, and threat intelligence. Unlike traditional security teams focused on monitoring alerts and responding to known threats, threat hunters are proactive, seeking out potential threats without predefined alerts or indicators.

Role of the Threat Hunter: Threat hunters need a mindset that combines creativity, critical thinking, and deep knowledge of adversary tactics and techniques. Their role involves creating hypotheses about potential threats, searching for abnormal activity, and working to detect unknown threats that could bypass automated defenses.

Building a Multi-Disciplinary Team: A well-rounded team typically includes members with diverse backgrounds in malware analysis, network security, and forensic analysis, among other areas. This diversity of expertise allows the team to approach threat hunting from multiple angles, from network traffic analysis to endpoint behavior monitoring.

Continuous Training and Development: The cyber threat landscape evolves rapidly, making it essential for threat hunters to stay updated on the latest adversary techniques, tools, and methodologies. Regular training, certifications, and exposure to new threat intelligence help ensure the team can adapt to emerging threats effectively.

3. Leveraging Threat Intelligence

Threat intelligence is a critical component of any threat hunting program, as it provides the context and knowledge necessary to understand current threats and adversary behaviors. High-quality threat intelligence enables hunters to anticipate and identify potential attacks more effectively, and it informs the hypotheses that guide their investigations.

Sources of Threat Intelligence: Threat hunters should leverage a variety of intelligence sources, including open-source threat feeds, private intelligence providers, and information shared by industry peers. Threat intelligence can also come from internal sources, such as data from past incidents or insights from other teams within the organization.

Using Intelligence to Formulate Hypotheses: Threat intelligence provides a foundation for formulating hypotheses. For example, if recent intelligence suggests a rise in phishing attacks targeting specific sectors, the threat hunting team may investigate suspicious email patterns or unusual login attempts, aiming to detect early signs of compromise.

Integrating Threat Intelligence into Workflows: Threat intelligence should be seamlessly integrated into threat-hunting workflows, enabling the team to apply relevant data to real-time investigations. Automated threat intelligence platforms can assist by regularly updating data feeds and integrating intelligence into existing security tools for quick reference.

4. Developing and Refining Hypotheses

The hypothesis-driven approach is central to threat hunting, allowing teams to proactively search for indicators of compromise based on educated guesses about potential threats. A well-formed hypothesis should be actionable, measurable, and focused on specific behaviors or tactics adversaries might use.

Creating Hypotheses Based on Known Threats: Hypotheses often stem from known adversary Tactics, Techniques, and Procedures (TTPs), or trends identified in threat intelligence. For instance, if an organization is aware of increased ransomware activity, hunters might investigate changes in network traffic indicative of ransomware installation or encryption.

Evaluating and Testing Hypotheses: Threat hunters need the tools and capabilities to test their hypotheses, either through direct data analysis or by deploying honeypots and sandbox environments to observe potential attack behaviors. Hypotheses are iterative, evolving based on the findings, which helps the team refine their focus and improve detection accuracy.

Continuous Hypothesis Generation: Threat hunters should continuously develop new hypotheses as they gain insights from investigations and learn about new adversarial tactics. This cycle of hypothesis creation, testing, and refinement forms the backbone of a proactive threat hunting program, keeping the team responsive to evolving threats.

5. Implementing and Managing Tools and Technologies

An effective threat hunting program relies on a range of tools that provide deep visibility into network and system activities. The selection of tools and technologies should align with the team's goals, giving them the ability to gather, analyze, and interpret data across the environment.

Key Tools for Threat Hunting: Essential tools include Security Information and Event Management (SIEM) systems, Endpoint Detection and Response (EDR) platforms, and Network Traffic Analysis (NTA) solutions. These tools allow threat hunters to monitor for abnormal activity, analyze logs, and correlate data across different sources.

Data Collection and Enrichment: Effective threat hunting requires access to comprehensive data sources, such as endpoint logs, network traffic, and user behavior analytics. Enriching this data with context, such as threat intelligence or information about normal operational patterns, helps hunters identify what's unusual and prioritize their investigations.

Automation and Customization: Many threat-hunting tasks can be enhanced with automation, such as filtering log data or flagging known malicious IPs. However, customization is equally important—hunters often need to tailor tools to detect unique behaviors or anomalies specific to their environment, which helps in capturing the subtle indicators that automated tools may miss.

6. Creating a Feedback Loop for Continuous Improvement

A threat-hunting program must be adaptive and continuously evolving, responding to new threats and refining its methods based on past experiences. Establishing a feedback loop ensures that lessons learned are integrated into future hunts, contributing to a cycle of continuous improvement.

Learning from Past Hunts: Each hunting engagement offers insights into the environment's vulnerabilities and adversarial tactics. By reviewing completed hunts, the team can identify what worked, what didn't, and where improvements are needed, making future hunts more efficient and effective.

Incorporating Findings into Security Policies: The findings from threat-hunting engagements often reveal areas where security policies or configurations need adjustment. By feeding these insights back into the organization's overall security strategy, the program strengthens its defenses and reduces the likelihood of future compromises.

Measuring Success and Adjusting Goals: Threat hunting success is often measured by metrics such as the time to detect threats, the number of identified anomalies, and reductions in dwell time. Regular assessment of these metrics allows teams to refine their approach, set new goals, and allocate resources more effectively.

Building a threat-hunting program requires more than just technology—it demands a proactive mindset, skilled personnel, and a clear strategic focus. With well-defined goals, a skilled team, actionable intelligence, and continuous improvement, organizations can develop a robust program that goes beyond passive defense. By embracing the essentials of threat hunting, organizations gain a proactive approach to security, increasing their resilience in an ever-evolving cyber threat landscape.

3.2 Assembling the Right Team

Creating an effective threat-hunting team is a foundational element in building a proactive cybersecurity strategy. A capable team brings together diverse skills, experiences, and mindsets essential for identifying and neutralizing threats that evade conventional defenses. This chapter explores the types of professionals required for a successful threat-hunting team, the roles they play, and strategies for recruiting and retaining top talent.

1. Core Roles in a Threat-Hunting Team

A threat-hunting team requires a range of expertise, with each member contributing unique skills that enable the team to anticipate, detect, and investigate potential threats. Here's an overview of key roles in a well-rounded threat-hunting team:

Threat Hunters: These cybersecurity experts specialize in identifying unknown or emerging threats within the organization's network. They work with hypotheses based on threat intelligence, using various tools to detect anomalies and malicious activities that automated systems may miss. Threat hunters often have strong analytical skills and a deep understanding of adversary tactics, techniques, and procedures (TTPs).

Malware Analysts: Malware analysts specialize in understanding and dissecting malware, identifying its structure, behavior, and potential impact on the organization. They can reverse-engineer malware, providing insights that help threat hunters recognize the signs of a breach or pinpoint specific vulnerabilities targeted by attackers.

Forensic Analysts: Forensic analysts focus on gathering and analyzing evidence of cyber incidents, preserving the chain of custody and helping to reconstruct attacker activity. Their skills are essential for examining compromised systems and gathering the evidence needed for remediation, response, and, potentially, legal action.

Network Security Engineers: These professionals bring deep expertise in network design, monitoring, and traffic analysis. They help identify network patterns and anomalies that may indicate unauthorized access or malicious behavior, enabling the team to secure vulnerable areas and detect lateral movement within the network.

Incident Response (IR) Specialists: Although they are often part of a separate team, having IR specialists within the threat-hunting team can enhance the program's overall effectiveness. They respond to confirmed incidents, execute containment strategies, and collaborate with threat hunters to apply real-time insights into ongoing investigations.

2. Skills and Competencies for Threat Hunters

Threat hunting requires a unique set of skills and a proactive mindset. While technical expertise is essential, the ability to think creatively and approach problems from multiple angles is equally important. Core skills include:

Analytical Thinking: Threat hunters must be able to analyze complex data sets, draw connections, and identify patterns that could signal potential threats. This involves a combination of statistical, behavioral, and anomaly detection techniques.

Knowledge of Adversary Tactics: A deep understanding of TTPs, especially as documented in frameworks like MITRE ATT&CK, is essential. Hunters who can anticipate adversary behavior can build more effective detection rules and identify malicious actions more quickly.

Proficiency with Security Tools: Threat hunters must be proficient in using various security tools, including SIEM systems, EDR platforms, and data analysis solutions. Skills in scripting languages (e.g., Python, PowerShell) allow hunters to create custom detection rules and automate repetitive tasks.

Creativity and Curiosity: Threat hunting goes beyond monitoring alerts—it's about proactively seeking out potential threats. A creative and inquisitive mindset helps threat hunters form unique hypotheses and explore unconventional avenues in their search for threats.

Collaboration and Communication: Threat hunting is a collaborative effort, requiring team members to communicate findings and work closely with other cybersecurity functions, like the IR and SOC teams. Clear communication is essential for sharing insights, educating others on emerging threats, and ensuring coordinated responses.

3. Building a Collaborative Team Culture

Creating a cohesive and effective threat-hunting team involves fostering a culture that values collaboration, ongoing learning, and a proactive approach to security. Important aspects of building a strong team culture include:

Encouraging Knowledge Sharing: Effective threat hunting relies on sharing insights across the team and broader organization. Regular knowledge-sharing sessions, like threat intelligence briefings or case study reviews, help team members stay informed about the latest techniques and reinforce collaborative learning.

Fostering a Proactive Mindset: Team members should be encouraged to take initiative, explore new avenues for threat detection, and challenge assumptions. A proactive approach involves continuously refining hypotheses, testing new detection methods, and embracing a mindset of constant improvement.

Promoting Continuous Learning: The cyber threat landscape is dynamic, and threat hunters need to stay updated on the latest developments in adversary tactics, emerging tools, and regulatory changes. Providing opportunities for continuous learning through training, certifications, and conference participation keeps the team well-prepared.

Developing Trust and Teamwork: Trust is essential in a high-stakes field like threat hunting, where accurate analysis and coordinated responses are critical. Encouraging open communication and creating a supportive environment where team members can ask for help or share ideas without hesitation strengthens the team's overall performance.

4. Recruitment and Retention Strategies

Given the shortage of skilled cybersecurity professionals, finding and retaining talent in threat hunting can be challenging. However, there are strategies that can help attract the right candidates and keep them engaged:

Hiring for Potential and Passion: While experience is valuable, hiring managers should also focus on candidates with a demonstrated passion for cybersecurity, curiosity, and a willingness to learn. Candidates with diverse backgrounds, such as data science, software engineering, or IT administration, often bring fresh perspectives that benefit the team.

Offering Competitive Compensation and Benefits: To attract skilled professionals in a competitive job market, organizations must offer competitive salaries and benefits. Threat hunters are in high demand, so organizations that provide comprehensive benefits, including opportunities for career development and flexible working arrangements, are more likely to retain talent.

Investing in Training and Development: Ongoing professional development is essential for threat hunters, who need to stay ahead of the latest threats and technologies. Investing in regular training, certifications, and mentoring not only benefits the organization but also demonstrates a commitment to the team's growth and professional advancement.

Providing Career Pathways: Creating a defined career path for threat hunters, with opportunities for progression to senior roles or specialized areas such as threat intelligence or malware analysis, enhances job satisfaction and reduces turnover. Threat hunters who see a clear path for advancement within the organization are more likely to stay long-term.

5. Leveraging Outsourced Support and Expertise

In some cases, organizations may supplement their internal threat-hunting team with outsourced expertise. This can be especially valuable for smaller organizations or those that need specialized skills on a temporary basis. Options for outsourced support include:

Managed Detection and Response (MDR) Services: MDR providers offer comprehensive threat detection and response services, enabling organizations to access advanced threat-hunting capabilities without building an internal team from scratch.

Consultants and Contracted Threat Hunters: Cybersecurity consultants can provide specific expertise or assist with large-scale investigations, especially during times of heightened threat activity. Engaging with consultants can help transfer knowledge to the internal team while handling complex cases.

Threat Intelligence Partners: Many organizations partner with threat intelligence providers, leveraging their expertise in tracking adversary behaviors, emerging threats, and relevant intelligence to inform internal threat-hunting efforts. This partnership enhances the internal team's capabilities and provides fresh insights into global threats.

6. Metrics for Measuring Team Performance

To ensure the threat-hunting team is effective, organizations should establish metrics for tracking and evaluating performance. Key metrics include:

Time to Detect and Respond: Reducing the time taken to detect and respond to threats is a core goal of any threat-hunting team. Tracking this metric helps measure efficiency and guides improvements in detection and response workflows.

Number and Quality of Threats Discovered: The volume and impact of threats discovered over time offer insight into the effectiveness of threat-hunting activities. Emphasis should be placed not only on quantity but on identifying high-impact threats and reducing false positives.

Hypotheses Tested and Results: Tracking the number of hypotheses tested and the results of each investigation can help determine the team's productivity and innovative capacity. Positive results can demonstrate the success of proactive detection, while unsuccessful hypotheses still provide learning opportunities.

Training and Skill Development: Measuring the progress of team members in training, certifications, and other skill development activities helps ensure the team's capabilities remain aligned with evolving threats. It also highlights the organization's commitment to professional development, which supports retention.

Assembling the right team is vital for creating a threat-hunting program that can anticipate and address sophisticated threats in real-time. By balancing technical skills with a collaborative culture and continuous learning, organizations can build a high-performing team that stays ahead of adversaries. With the right roles, recruitment strategies, and performance metrics in place, the threat-hunting team becomes an invaluable asset, enhancing the organization's resilience in an ever-changing cyber threat landscape.

3.3 Choosing a Framework

Selecting the right framework for threat hunting is critical to creating a structured, repeatable, and effective process that aligns with an organization's unique security needs. Frameworks offer structured guidelines and best practices that threat-hunting teams can use to standardize processes, identify gaps, and enhance detection strategies. This chapter explores various popular frameworks, such as MITRE ATT&CK, the Cyber Kill Chain, and Diamond Model, explaining how each can be applied in threat hunting and how to select the best fit for a specific threat-hunting program.

1. The Role of Frameworks in Threat Hunting

Frameworks provide a roadmap for threat-hunting teams, offering step-by-step guidelines that clarify each stage of the threat-hunting process. They help teams avoid ad hoc methods, which can be inconsistent or ineffective, by creating a shared approach that standardizes threat-hunting activities. In this way, frameworks support efficiency, ensure consistency, and allow teams to build a record of processes and findings, making it easier to learn from previous hunts and improve over time.

Standardizing Detection Methods: A framework can help threat hunters use common definitions and procedures, ensuring everyone on the team interprets events similarly and reducing the likelihood of false positives or missed threats.

Guiding Hypothesis Development: Frameworks help structure how hunters develop hypotheses, organize investigations, and collect evidence by offering established patterns of adversarial behavior that hunters can anticipate and search for.

Supporting Communication and Reporting: Frameworks facilitate clear reporting and communication with other cybersecurity functions by creating a standardized language for describing threat behaviors, vulnerabilities, and hunting successes or needs for improvement.

2. MITRE ATT&CK Framework

The MITRE ATT&CK framework has become one of the most widely adopted frameworks in threat hunting, valued for its comprehensive, real-world mapping of adversary tactics, techniques, and procedures (TTPs). It categorizes malicious activities into a matrix of tactics and techniques that adversaries use to penetrate systems and evade detection, providing a powerful reference for threat hunters to anticipate and investigate specific threats.

Mapping Adversary Behavior: ATT&CK maps out a range of known behaviors, from initial access to command and control, that adversaries may use to infiltrate and compromise systems. This model allows hunters to look for indicators tied to specific tactics, such as credential dumping or lateral movement, that adversaries may attempt.

Creating Focused Hypotheses: Using ATT&CK, hunters can design specific hypotheses based on observed behaviors, past incidents, or intelligence suggesting that a particular adversary tactic is on the rise. For example, if lateral movement techniques are prevalent, a hypothesis might target unusual patterns in network traffic between high-value assets.

Using ATT&CK for Threat Detection Rules: ATT&CK can help structure detection rules across an organization's monitoring tools, ensuring that threat-hunting activities and automated detections align with the latest adversary techniques. By prioritizing ATT&CK techniques known to target the organization's assets, the team can improve both proactive and reactive threat detection.

3. The Cyber Kill Chain

Developed by Lockheed Martin, the Cyber Kill Chain framework breaks down an attack into seven stages, from reconnaissance to data exfiltration, illustrating how adversaries progress through each step to reach their objectives. This model is useful for understanding the lifecycle of attacks and provides a basis for intercepting threats at various stages.

Tracking Attack Progression: By understanding where adversaries are likely to move next in the kill chain, threat hunters can more effectively predict subsequent actions. For instance, if malware is detected at the installation phase, hunters can focus on identifying command and control channels or signs of lateral movement.

Intervening at Key Points: The Cyber Kill Chain emphasizes intercepting threats at different points within the chain, so hunters can design hunts that target specific phases, such as delivery (phishing attempts) or installation (malware on endpoints). Preventing an attack from progressing to the next phase can reduce overall risk.

Use in Threat Mitigation Strategy: Integrating the kill chain approach with other tools, like SIEM or EDR, allows teams to correlate events that may indicate different phases of an attack, enabling earlier detection and response. This model is especially valuable when applied alongside threat intelligence that provides insights into adversary-specific patterns.

4. The Diamond Model of Intrusion Analysis

The Diamond Model of Intrusion Analysis offers a unique perspective by examining the relationships between four key elements: the adversary, their capabilities, the victim, and the infrastructure used. This model is particularly useful in targeted threat hunting, as it enables a deeper understanding of the relationships and motivations behind an attack.

Focusing on Attack Relationships: The Diamond Model helps hunters understand how each component of an attack relates to the others, focusing on connections like how an adversary leverages infrastructure to target specific vulnerabilities. This perspective can guide hunters to explore how or why specific targets are at risk.

Hypothesis Generation Based on Adversary Patterns: Threat hunters can leverage the model to hypothesize how adversaries might adapt or reuse infrastructure to exploit similar targets. For example, observing a consistent pattern in phishing infrastructure across multiple campaigns could lead hunters to explore additional phishing attempts targeting specific teams or employees.

Mapping Out Threat Actor Profiles: This model is highly beneficial for profiling specific adversaries, particularly those who repeatedly target the organization. By studying attacker patterns, teams can build more focused defenses and recognize specific TTPs that indicate the presence of a known threat actor.

5. Selecting the Right Framework for Your Organization

Each framework has strengths that make it suited to different threat-hunting needs. Choosing the most suitable framework—or combining multiple frameworks—depends on an organization's unique risk landscape, security goals, and available resources.

Assessing Organizational Threat Landscape: The choice of framework should reflect the organization's primary risks. For instance, if the organization faces targeted attacks from specific adversaries, the Diamond Model may offer a better fit. Alternatively, for organizations that need to comprehensively map adversary techniques across their systems, the MITRE ATT&CK framework may be more appropriate.

Aligning Frameworks with Security Maturity Level: Organizations with mature cybersecurity programs may benefit from combining frameworks, such as using the Cyber Kill Chain to map out attack phases while employing ATT&CK to detect specific adversary techniques at each stage. Smaller organizations or those early in threat hunting may choose to start with a single framework and expand as capabilities develop.

Resource Availability and Team Expertise: Threat-hunting frameworks can vary in complexity and data requirements. ATT&CK, for instance, requires substantial logging and monitoring data to correlate techniques effectively, which may demand advanced infrastructure and skilled analysts. Organizations should select frameworks that align with their team's capabilities, ensuring they can apply it effectively without overextending resources.

6. Implementing and Customizing Frameworks

Once a framework is selected, teams should adapt it to their specific operational environment. Customizing frameworks ensures they align with organizational requirements, assets, and potential adversary behaviors, making the framework more actionable and effective in the organization's unique context.

Integrating Frameworks with Detection Tools: Many frameworks, such as ATT&CK, offer integration points with SIEM, EDR, and threat intelligence platforms. Customizing these integrations can automate data collection and correlation, making it easier for threat hunters to connect observed behaviors to specific tactics or stages in an attack lifecycle.

Tailoring Frameworks to Organizational Assets: Threat-hunting frameworks should reflect the organization's critical assets, data flows, and known threat actor profiles. Tailoring frameworks to focus on high-value assets or prioritize techniques used against similar organizations improves relevance and results.

Regularly Updating and Refining Frameworks: As threat tactics evolve, frameworks should be reviewed and updated to ensure ongoing effectiveness. This includes incorporating insights from recent threat intelligence, adapting to new attacker TTPs, and continuously enhancing detection rules based on past findings.

Choosing the right threat-hunting framework is a pivotal step in developing a proactive, effective threat-hunting program. Whether the organization chooses the widely adopted MITRE ATT&CK, the Cyber Kill Chain for lifecycle insights, or the relational Diamond Model, the framework selected should align with its specific risk landscape and security goals. By implementing frameworks thoughtfully and customizing them to reflect the organization's unique context, threat hunters can optimize their approach, improve detection, and build a more resilient defense against evolving cyber threats.

4. Threat Intelligence and Its Role in Threat Hunting

Threat intelligence is a cornerstone of effective cyber threat hunting, providing the contextual information and insights necessary to identify and mitigate risks before they escalate into incidents. In this chapter, we will explore the various types of threat intelligence—strategic, operational, tactical, and technical—and their unique contributions to the threat hunting process. We will discuss how to integrate threat intelligence into hunting strategies, enabling hunters to make informed decisions based on real-time data about adversary tactics, techniques, and procedures (TTPs). Additionally, we will examine the sources of threat intelligence, including open-source and commercial feeds, and emphasize the importance of evaluating and validating intelligence to ensure its reliability. By leveraging threat intelligence effectively, organizations can enhance their hunting efforts, anticipate potential threats, and strengthen their overall security posture.

4.1 Understanding Different Types of Threat Intelligence

Threat intelligence plays an essential role in a successful threat-hunting program by offering insights into potential adversaries, their methods, and the tactics they may use to target organizations. However, effective use of threat intelligence requires understanding the different types of threat intelligence, as each serves a unique purpose and provides value in different ways. In this chapter, we will cover the primary types of threat intelligence—strategic, tactical, operational, and technical—and explain how each can be applied to enhance threat-hunting efforts.

1. Strategic Threat Intelligence

Strategic threat intelligence focuses on understanding the broad, overarching trends in cybersecurity threats and adversary tactics. It is typically presented in a high-level format and designed for an executive or managerial audience, helping them make informed decisions about risk management and cybersecurity investments. Strategic intelligence is less about immediate response and more about building long-term strategies.

Content and Format: Strategic intelligence includes information about global or sector-specific threat trends, emerging adversaries, and the evolving threat landscape. It's often presented through white papers, annual threat reports, and intelligence briefs, summarizing key findings without excessive technical detail.

Purpose for Threat Hunting: While not directly actionable for hunting specific threats, strategic intelligence provides context for what the organization may face, allowing threat hunters to prioritize areas of interest based on larger patterns and likely targets. For instance, if strategic intelligence reports highlight increased attacks on healthcare data, healthcare organizations might prioritize threat hunting around data theft or ransomware targeting patient records.

Examples: An organization might consult strategic intelligence from sources like industry threat reports, government agencies (such as CISA or ENISA), or intelligence providers that track adversarial trends across industries. These insights can guide decision-making, influence security budgets, and help formulate broad security policies.

2. Tactical Threat Intelligence

Tactical threat intelligence provides a more granular look at adversaries' methods, tools, and techniques. It includes information on the specific TTPs (Tactics, Techniques, and Procedures) that adversaries use to compromise systems and evade detection. This intelligence is especially useful for guiding technical defenses and hunting activities, as it offers detailed insights into adversary methods.

Content and Format: Tactical intelligence covers the specific techniques adversaries use at different stages of an attack, aligned with frameworks like MITRE ATT&CK. This might include known phishing techniques, tools for lateral movement, or common privilege escalation methods. Tactical intelligence is often shared as alerts, advisories, or structured in matrices like ATT&CK, which catalog adversary behaviors for hunters to map and reference.

Purpose for Threat Hunting: Tactical intelligence is actionable and directly relevant to threat hunters. It allows hunters to search for specific indicators within their environments that could indicate an adversary's presence, such as unusual login patterns or abnormal file access behaviors associated with credential theft. By aligning their activities with documented TTPs, threat hunters can more effectively target specific adversary behaviors.

Examples: A tactical threat intelligence feed might alert hunters to specific remote access tools being deployed by a well-known hacking group. With this knowledge, hunters can develop hypotheses around access points and privilege escalation techniques and prioritize hunting activities that correlate with these adversarial patterns.

3. Operational Threat Intelligence

Operational threat intelligence, also known as technical intelligence, provides information about specific cyber events, incidents, or campaigns. This intelligence is typically more time-sensitive and is often delivered in near-real-time to alert organizations about active threats that could directly impact their operations. Operational intelligence is valuable for threat hunters seeking to proactively identify and mitigate specific threats that have recently targeted similar organizations.

Content and Format: Operational intelligence details indicators of compromise (IOCs), such as IP addresses, file hashes, or domains known to be associated with a particular campaign. This intelligence is time-sensitive and can include real-time reports, bulletins, and alerts sent to the organization's security operations team to prompt immediate actions.

Purpose for Threat Hunting: Operational intelligence allows threat hunters to search for recent indicators within their systems that may reveal an ongoing attack or campaign. By comparing current activities against known IOCs, hunters can quickly identify and respond to specific threats targeting their sector or organization. Operational intelligence enables rapid response, helping teams prevent further escalation and contain any active threats.

Examples: If operational intelligence reports an active phishing campaign using a specific domain and IP range, hunters can proactively search for traffic associated with these IOCs within their network logs. This can help the organization detect potential compromises and block access to these domains before significant damage occurs.

4. Technical Threat Intelligence

Technical threat intelligence offers granular, highly specific information on the mechanisms and artifacts of an attack. This form of intelligence is primarily geared toward identifying technical indicators, such as malicious file signatures, registry keys, and command-and-control (C2) infrastructure. Technical intelligence provides insights into how specific malware operates or how certain exploits function, making it directly actionable for threat-hunting activities focused on detection.

Content and Format: Technical intelligence includes details on IOCs, malware signatures, command-and-control (C2) server IPs, and exploit code. This intelligence is shared through feeds and reports containing malware analysis, code snippets, and specific technical artifacts.

Purpose for Threat Hunting: Technical threat intelligence is used by threat hunters to create detection rules and to look for specific indicators associated with known malware or exploits. Hunters can use these details to conduct a more focused search within their network, looking for matching signatures, behavior patterns, or exploit indicators that could reveal hidden adversaries.

Examples: For example, technical intelligence may reveal that a particular malware strain communicates with a specific C2 IP. Hunters can then search for this IP in network traffic logs or develop YARA rules based on malware file signatures, enhancing their ability to detect and isolate infected systems.

5. Integrating Different Types of Threat Intelligence

Effective threat hunting often involves combining multiple types of threat intelligence to develop a comprehensive view of the adversary landscape. Strategic intelligence provides high-level trends that help set the organization's overall focus, while tactical and operational intelligence give direct guidance on where and how to look for specific adversary behaviors. Technical intelligence provides the fine-grained details required to detect and analyze malicious artifacts.

Creating a Threat Intelligence Framework: By aligning each type of threat intelligence with specific goals and tools, organizations can ensure that intelligence is effectively integrated across different security operations functions. For instance, strategic intelligence might inform long-term threat-hunting priorities, while operational intelligence can prompt immediate investigative actions.

Using Threat Intelligence Platforms (TIPs): TIPs can help aggregate, correlate, and manage threat intelligence from various sources, allowing hunters to leverage multiple intelligence types simultaneously. By automating this process, TIPs make it easier for hunters to track known IOCs, connect observed behaviors to broader trends, and quickly respond to emerging threats.

Refining Hypotheses with Intelligence: Threat hunters can leverage intelligence to build stronger, data-backed hypotheses. For example, strategic intelligence may suggest that ransomware is a rising risk in their industry, while tactical intelligence highlights a specific ransomware variant. Operational intelligence may then reveal current IOCs for that variant, allowing hunters to search for active signs of compromise.

Understanding the different types of threat intelligence and how they interconnect is essential for threat-hunting teams to make informed decisions and maximize their effectiveness. By strategically integrating strategic, tactical, operational, and technical intelligence, hunters can target specific adversary behaviors, proactively detect emerging threats, and enhance overall resilience. With a strong foundation in threat intelligence, threat-hunting teams can better anticipate adversary actions, respond swiftly to incidents, and ultimately, fortify the organization against an ever-evolving cyber threat landscape.

4.2 Integrating Threat Intelligence in the Hunt

Integrating threat intelligence into threat hunting transforms data on threats into actionable insights, guiding hunters to locate and neutralize threats with greater precision and speed. By embedding threat intelligence into each stage of the hunt, security teams can proactively focus on high-priority threats, build hypotheses rooted in real-world adversary behavior, and quickly identify indicators of compromise (IOCs). This chapter explores how to effectively incorporate strategic, tactical, operational, and technical threat intelligence into the threat-hunting process, emphasizing methods to leverage intelligence for more efficient detection, analysis, and response.

1. Using Threat Intelligence for Hypothesis Development

Hypothesis development is the foundation of a successful threat hunt, and threat intelligence offers critical insights that can guide and refine these hypotheses. By understanding current adversarial tactics, techniques, and procedures (TTPs), hunters can design hunts around likely attack methods that may already be present within their networks.

Leveraging Tactical Intelligence for Hypothesis Building: Tactical intelligence, which includes adversary TTPs, helps hunters anticipate how attackers might attempt to exploit weaknesses or target specific assets. For example, if intelligence reveals that ransomware groups frequently use phishing to gain initial access, a hypothesis can focus on abnormal email interactions or credential use in sensitive areas.

Operational Intelligence to Address Emerging Threats: Operational intelligence on active threat campaigns can inform hypotheses that are directly relevant to recent or ongoing attacks. For example, if a specific threat actor is targeting the financial sector with remote access trojans (RATs), hunters can develop hypotheses that explore unusual outbound connections associated with RAT command-and-control (C2) channels.

Strategic Intelligence for High-Level Focus Areas: Although strategic intelligence is broader, it can be used to set the overarching focus areas for threat-hunting operations. For example, if strategic intelligence suggests that the organization's industry faces increased ransomware risks, threat hunters can prioritize hunts that target ransomware behaviors, file encryption patterns, or lateral movement.

2. Enhancing Data Collection and Enrichment

Threat intelligence provides contextual details that enhance the data collection phase of the hunt, allowing threat hunters to enrich data sources with known indicators and adversary behaviors. By correlating internal data with external intelligence, hunters can more accurately pinpoint potential threats and eliminate noise.

Enriching Logs with Indicators of Compromise (IOCs): Integrating operational and technical intelligence into log analysis can reveal known IOCs such as malicious IP addresses, file hashes, or URLs. When threat hunters run searches, the enriched logs make it easier to spot connections between network activities and known malicious indicators, expediting the hunt.

Threat Intelligence Platforms (TIPs) for Aggregation: Many organizations use TIPs to aggregate and correlate threat intelligence from multiple sources. TIPs automatically enrich logs with known threat data, providing a centralized repository of intelligence for use in the hunt. For example, hunters can query enriched log data directly for recent phishing IOCs identified by operational intelligence feeds.

Using Intelligence to Prioritize Data Sources: Threat intelligence helps prioritize which data sources hunters should focus on. If, for instance, intelligence indicates that malware is spreading through email attachments, hunters can focus on email logs, sandboxed attachment analysis, and email filtering solutions as primary sources for data collection.

3. Tailoring Detection Techniques with Threat Intelligence

Effective detection hinges on understanding how adversaries operate, and threat intelligence equips hunters with this knowledge. By aligning detection methods with TTPs, IOCs, and known adversary strategies, threat hunters can set up more targeted and accurate alerts, reducing false positives and capturing relevant events.

Mapping to the MITRE ATT&CK Framework: The MITRE ATT&CK framework is invaluable for leveraging tactical intelligence, as it categorizes adversary TTPs into structured matrices. Hunters can match intelligence-based TTPs to MITRE's tactics and techniques, then search for these behaviors within their environment. For example, if a threat actor often uses "Credential Dumping," hunters can prioritize techniques under the "Credential Access" tactic.

Customizing Detection Rules with Technical Intelligence: Technical threat intelligence offers IOCs such as file hashes and C2 server IPs that can be fed into SIEMs and Endpoint Detection and Response (EDR) tools to create tailored detection rules. Hunters can adjust thresholds and conditions based on intelligence, improving detection of specific threats without overwhelming teams with non-relevant alerts.

Real-Time Threat Detection with Operational Intelligence Feeds: Operational intelligence can feed into real-time monitoring systems to identify ongoing attack campaigns. For example, if a new zero-day vulnerability is being actively exploited, hunters can configure detection rules that focus on network traffic or behaviors associated with the exploit, allowing for a faster response.

4. Refining Threat Hunting with Contextual Intelligence

Understanding the context around potential threats can make threat-hunting efforts far more effective. Threat intelligence provides context on threat actors, typical victim profiles, and specific adversarial goals, helping hunters prioritize hunts around the organization's most relevant risks.

Assessing Threat Actor Profiles and Motivations: Strategic and tactical intelligence may include profiles of threat actors that target similar organizations. If intelligence suggests a financially motivated group is active in the industry, hunters can tailor searches to focus on techniques that align with data theft or financial gain.

Contextualizing Alerts with Historical Data: When an alert matches an IOC from operational or technical intelligence, hunters can use the context provided by intelligence sources to determine the threat's relevance and priority. For example, a malicious IP match might be deprioritized if it is associated with older malware that lacks the capacity for advanced attacks.

Correlating with Environmental Factors: Threat intelligence can indicate if certain threats are more active in specific regions or industries. For example, if a report highlights increased state-sponsored attacks in a certain region, threat hunters may prioritize hunts around techniques associated with espionage, such as credential harvesting or data exfiltration, in the affected areas.

5. Responding and Reporting with Threat Intelligence Insights

Once a potential threat is identified, threat intelligence continues to play a key role by informing the response and supporting comprehensive reporting. Intelligence on adversary tactics, goals, and possible follow-up actions helps hunters respond more effectively and communicate their findings with a detailed understanding of the threat.

Intelligence-Driven Response Actions: Threat intelligence on adversary tactics can guide response actions, such as isolating specific assets or disabling compromised accounts. For example, if intelligence indicates that a threat actor often deploys a secondary payload following credential theft, the response may prioritize additional scans on critical systems for potential secondary infections.

Creating Detailed Incident Reports: Using threat intelligence in reporting helps communicate the full context and scope of a threat to stakeholders. A report enriched with intelligence on the adversary's known TTPs, attack goals, and recent campaign activities provides a comprehensive view, supporting better decision-making and future preventative measures.

Feedback Loop for Continuous Improvement: After a hunt or incident response, intelligence should be fed back into the threat-hunting cycle. Insights from the incident can refine intelligence feeds and detection mechanisms, ensuring continuous improvement in both the quality of intelligence and hunting effectiveness.

6. Best Practices for Effective Threat Intelligence Integration

Maximizing the value of threat intelligence in threat hunting requires a systematic approach, where intelligence is not only used as supplementary data but integrated as a core part of the hunting methodology. Here are some best practices for effective integration:

Automate Intelligence Enrichment Where Possible: Automation tools can streamline intelligence integration, reducing manual work and ensuring data is consistently enriched with the latest indicators and contextual insights. Automated enrichment can feed directly into SIEM or EDR systems, improving real-time threat detection capabilities.

Establish Threat Intelligence Prioritization: Not all intelligence is equally valuable; prioritize intelligence feeds that are most relevant to your organization's industry, threat landscape, and risk appetite. Focus on intelligence providers that offer frequent updates on adversaries that target similar sectors.

Regularly Update Detection Rules and Techniques: Threat intelligence is constantly evolving as adversaries adapt, making it essential to regularly update detection rules, hunting methodologies, and intelligence integrations. This ongoing refinement ensures hunters stay up-to-date with the latest adversary tactics and techniques.

Foster Collaboration Across Security Teams: Collaboration between threat hunters, intelligence analysts, and incident responders maximizes the effectiveness of intelligence. Intelligence analysts can provide hunters with real-time insights, while hunters can inform analysts of newly observed patterns, creating a synergistic approach to security.

Integrating threat intelligence into the threat-hunting process allows security teams to stay one step ahead of adversaries, transforming intelligence into a tactical asset that guides proactive threat identification and rapid incident response. By leveraging each type of intelligence—from broad strategic insights to specific technical indicators—hunters can build hypotheses, prioritize detection, and conduct contextualized hunts that reveal potential threats more effectively. With a structured approach to intelligence integration, organizations can continuously improve their threat-hunting capabilities, strengthening their overall resilience against an ever-evolving cyber threat landscape.

4.3 Sourcing and Evaluating Threat Intelligence

The effectiveness of a threat-hunting program significantly relies on the quality and relevance of the threat intelligence it utilizes. Threat intelligence is abundant, coming from diverse sources—ranging from commercial vendors to open-source platforms. However, not all threat intelligence is created equal, and organizations must develop a structured approach to sourcing and evaluating intelligence. This chapter delves into best practices for sourcing high-quality threat intelligence, evaluating its credibility and relevance, and integrating it effectively into the threat-hunting process.

1. Types of Threat Intelligence Sources

Understanding the various sources of threat intelligence is crucial for building a comprehensive threat landscape. The main categories of threat intelligence sources include:

Commercial Vendors: These are organizations that specialize in cybersecurity intelligence and offer curated feeds, reports, and analysis. Commercial vendors often provide proprietary data, advanced analytics, and dedicated threat research teams. Organizations can access intelligence from these vendors through subscription-based models. Examples include FireEye, CrowdStrike, and Recorded Future.

Open Source Intelligence (OSINT): OSINT refers to publicly available information, which can include blogs, forums, security websites, social media, and government reports. OSINT can be valuable for gathering insights into emerging threats, malware samples, or indicators associated with recent attacks. Platforms like VirusTotal and Hybrid Analysis provide access to valuable OSINT resources.

Information Sharing and Analysis Centers (ISACs): ISACs are industry-specific organizations that facilitate information sharing among member organizations. They collect and disseminate threat intelligence relevant to specific sectors, allowing organizations to learn from shared experiences. Membership in an ISAC can provide timely alerts and insights from peers facing similar threats.

Government Agencies: Government entities, such as the Cybersecurity and Infrastructure Security Agency (CISA) and the European Union Agency for Cybersecurity (ENISA), publish threat intelligence reports, advisories, and alerts. These resources often cover national or international threats and can be especially relevant for organizations operating in sensitive industries.

Community and Collaborative Platforms: Platforms like MISP (Malware Information Sharing Platform) allow organizations to share threat intelligence within communities. Collaboration in these platforms can provide access to valuable insights and IOCs that may not be available through other channels.

2. Criteria for Evaluating Threat Intelligence

To ensure that the threat intelligence gathered is actionable and relevant, organizations should establish criteria for evaluating the quality and credibility of their sources. Key criteria include:

Source Credibility: Assess the reputation and reliability of the source providing the intelligence. Established commercial vendors and government agencies typically offer higher credibility than anonymous or unverified sources. Reviewing the provider's track record, methodologies, and past performance can help determine reliability.

Relevance: Evaluate how pertinent the intelligence is to the organization's specific context. Intelligence that addresses threats relevant to the organization's industry, geographic region, and technology stack will be far more valuable. For example, intelligence focused on ransomware would be particularly relevant to organizations in sectors heavily targeted by these attacks.

Timeliness: Threat intelligence must be timely to be actionable. Evaluate how frequently the source updates its intelligence and whether the information reflects the latest threats and trends. Real-time or near-real-time feeds are particularly valuable for detecting active threats.

Actionability: Assess whether the intelligence can be directly applied in the threat-hunting process. Actionable intelligence includes specific IOCs, recommended detection methods, and clear indicators that can inform hunts. Intelligence that lacks specific details or is overly vague may not provide immediate utility.

Granularity: The level of detail provided by the intelligence source can influence its applicability. For instance, intelligence that includes specific TTPs (Tactics, Techniques, and Procedures), detailed IOCs, or contextual data on threat actors can enhance the threat-hunting process more effectively than broader, high-level information.

3. Sourcing Threat Intelligence Effectively

To maximize the benefits of threat intelligence in threat hunting, organizations should follow best practices for sourcing intelligence:

Diversify Intelligence Sources: Relying on a single source can create blind spots in threat visibility. Organizations should aim to source intelligence from a mix of commercial, open-source, government, and collaborative platforms. This diversity provides a broader perspective on emerging threats and enhances situational awareness.

Leverage Automation for Collection: Automated tools can streamline the collection of threat intelligence, allowing security teams to focus on analysis rather than manual data gathering. Threat intelligence platforms (TIPs) can help aggregate data from multiple sources, enrich it with contextual information, and present it in a usable format.

Participate in Information Sharing: Engaging with ISACs and community-driven platforms can provide organizations with access to timely and relevant intelligence. Sharing experiences with peer organizations and learning from their insights enhances collective cybersecurity defenses.

Maintain Strong Relationships with Vendors: Building relationships with threat intelligence vendors can lead to better service and tailored intelligence feeds. Open communication about specific organizational needs can help vendors provide more relevant insights and timely alerts.

4. Evaluating Threat Intelligence Effectiveness

Once threat intelligence has been sourced and integrated into the threat-hunting process, organizations should continuously evaluate its effectiveness. Key approaches include:

Feedback Mechanisms: Establish feedback loops between threat hunters and intelligence sources. Hunters can provide insights on which intelligence was actionable or effective in detecting threats. This feedback can inform future intelligence sourcing and enhance the quality of the intelligence received.

Regular Review and Analysis: Conduct periodic reviews of the threat intelligence used in past hunts. Analyzing outcomes—such as successful detections or false positives—can help identify patterns in which sources or types of intelligence were most useful.

Performance Metrics: Define and track metrics that measure the impact of threat intelligence on hunting outcomes. Metrics might include the speed of threat detection, the accuracy of alerts, and the correlation between intelligence-driven hunts and identified threats. Analyzing these metrics can highlight areas for improvement in intelligence sourcing and integration.

5. Challenges in Sourcing and Evaluating Threat Intelligence

Organizations face several challenges in sourcing and evaluating threat intelligence effectively:

Overabundance of Information: The sheer volume of threat intelligence available can overwhelm security teams. Filtering through large amounts of data to find relevant, actionable intelligence requires significant resources and can lead to information fatigue.

Quality vs. Quantity: Focusing too much on acquiring large volumes of intelligence may lead to reduced quality. Security teams should prioritize sourcing high-quality, relevant intelligence over simply increasing the amount of information gathered.

Dynamic Threat Landscape: The rapidly evolving nature of cyber threats makes it challenging to keep intelligence updated and relevant. Organizations must stay vigilant about emerging threats and trends while ensuring their intelligence remains aligned with the changing landscape.

Integration Complexity: Integrating diverse intelligence sources can present technical challenges, especially if data formats vary widely or if intelligence is not easily compatible with existing security systems. Organizations must invest in the right tools and processes to ensure smooth integration.

Sourcing and evaluating threat intelligence are critical components of an effective threat-hunting program. By diversifying sources, establishing clear evaluation criteria, and integrating intelligence into the hunting process, organizations can enhance their ability to detect and respond to threats proactively. Continuous evaluation and adaptation of intelligence strategies ensure that organizations remain vigilant and resilient against an ever-evolving cyber threat landscape. By leveraging high-quality threat intelligence, security teams can improve their overall threat-hunting effectiveness and better safeguard their organizations from potential attacks.

5. Tools and Technologies for Threat Hunting

The landscape of cyber threat hunting is heavily influenced by the tools and technologies available to security teams, which can significantly enhance their effectiveness and efficiency. In this chapter, we will explore the essential tools that form the backbone of a robust threat hunting program, including Security Information and Event Management (SIEM) systems, Endpoint Detection and Response (EDR) solutions, and Intrusion Detection Systems (IDS). We will delve into the advantages of each tool, discussing how they aid in data collection, analysis, and incident detection. Additionally, we will examine the transformative role of automation and artificial intelligence in threat hunting, highlighting how these technologies can streamline workflows and identify threats at unprecedented speeds. Finally, we will compare open-source tools with commercial solutions, helping readers understand the benefits and limitations of each. By equipping yourself with the right tools and technologies, you can empower your threat hunting initiatives and respond more effectively to the evolving threat landscape.

5.1 Core Tools of the Trade

In the realm of cyber threat hunting, having the right tools is essential for effectively detecting, analyzing, and responding to threats. These tools enable threat hunters to collect and analyze vast amounts of data, correlate findings, and automate processes to streamline investigations. This chapter explores the core tools of the trade, categorizing them into various types and discussing their functions, benefits, and importance in the threat-hunting lifecycle.

1. Security Information and Event Management (SIEM) Systems

SIEM systems are critical for aggregating, analyzing, and correlating security events from multiple sources within an organization. They serve as a centralized platform for security data collection and enable threat hunters to detect anomalies and potential threats through log analysis and alerting mechanisms.

Data Aggregation and Normalization: SIEM tools collect data from various sources, including firewalls, intrusion detection systems, servers, and endpoint devices. They normalize this data to provide a consistent format for analysis.

Real-Time Monitoring and Alerts: SIEM systems offer real-time monitoring capabilities, allowing threat hunters to identify suspicious activities as they occur. Configurable alerts help prioritize potential threats based on defined rules and thresholds.

Advanced Analytics and Correlation: Many SIEM solutions incorporate advanced analytics, such as machine learning and behavioral analysis, to detect patterns and correlations that may indicate a security incident. These capabilities enhance threat detection accuracy and reduce false positives.

2. Endpoint Detection and Response (EDR) Tools

EDR tools focus on monitoring and securing endpoints—laptops, desktops, servers, and other devices connected to the network. They provide threat hunters with visibility into endpoint activities, enabling rapid detection and response to potential threats.

Continuous Monitoring: EDR solutions continuously monitor endpoint activities, capturing detailed telemetry data, including process execution, file changes, and network connections. This visibility is crucial for identifying anomalous behaviors indicative of threats.

Threat Detection and Response: EDR tools employ various detection techniques, such as behavioral analysis, signature-based detection, and heuristic analysis, to identify malicious activities. They also facilitate incident response by allowing security teams to isolate or remediate compromised endpoints.

Forensics Capabilities: EDR tools often include forensic capabilities, enabling threat hunters to conduct deep dives into endpoint activities during and after an incident. Forensic analysis provides insights into the attack vector, tactics used, and impact on the organization.

3. Threat Intelligence Platforms (TIPs)

TIPs play a crucial role in aggregating and managing threat intelligence from various sources, allowing organizations to contextualize threats and enhance their threat-hunting efforts. They provide a centralized repository for storing, analyzing, and disseminating threat intelligence data.

Aggregation of Threat Intelligence Feeds: TIPs collect intelligence from multiple sources, including commercial vendors, open-source feeds, and community contributions. This aggregation provides a holistic view of the threat landscape.

Contextualization and Enrichment: TIPs enrich threat intelligence by providing context around indicators of compromise (IOCs), tactics, techniques, and procedures (TTPs), and threat actors. This contextualization helps hunters prioritize investigations based on relevance and potential impact.

Integration with Security Tools: TIPs can integrate with other security tools, such as SIEM and EDR solutions, to enhance detection and response capabilities. Automated ingestion of threat intelligence into these systems allows for faster and more informed decision-making.

4. Network Traffic Analysis (NTA) Tools

NTA tools focus on monitoring network traffic to identify suspicious activities, anomalies, and potential threats. They analyze network packets, connections, and communications between devices to detect malicious behaviors.

Deep Packet Inspection: NTA tools use deep packet inspection (DPI) to analyze the contents of network packets, enabling detection of known and unknown threats within network traffic.

Behavioral Analysis: Many NTA solutions employ behavioral analysis techniques to establish baselines of normal network activity. Any deviations from this baseline can trigger alerts for further investigation.

Threat Correlation: NTA tools can correlate network events with other security data, such as logs from SIEM or EDR solutions, to provide a comprehensive view of potential threats and facilitate incident response.

5. Malware Analysis Tools

Malware analysis tools are essential for understanding malicious code and its behavior. These tools allow threat hunters to dissect and analyze malware samples to identify their functionality, origins, and potential impact.

Static and Dynamic Analysis: Malware analysis tools can conduct static analysis (examining code without execution) and dynamic analysis (observing behavior during execution) to gain insights into malware capabilities and techniques.

Sandboxing Solutions: Many malware analysis tools offer sandbox environments where malware can be executed safely without affecting the broader network. This environment enables researchers to observe the malware's behavior, communication patterns, and potential targets.

Signature Generation and Threat Attribution: By analyzing malware samples, threat hunters can develop signatures to detect similar threats in the future. Additionally, analyzing indicators from malware can help attribute the threat to specific adversaries or campaigns.

6. Forensic Analysis Tools

Forensic analysis tools are critical for investigating and responding to security incidents. They enable threat hunters to examine compromised systems, recover evidence, and conduct post-incident analysis.

Disk and Memory Forensics: These tools allow threat hunters to analyze disk images and memory dumps to uncover artifacts, traces of malicious activity, and indicators of compromise.

File Recovery and Analysis: Forensic tools can recover deleted files and analyze them for evidence of malicious activity. This capability is crucial for understanding the extent of an attack and recovering lost data.

Timeline Reconstruction: Forensic analysis tools can help reconstruct timelines of events during a security incident. Understanding the sequence of actions can reveal attack methods and inform response strategies.

7. Incident Response Tools

Incident response tools assist organizations in managing security incidents effectively and efficiently. These tools facilitate coordination among response teams, track incidents, and document response activities.

Incident Management Systems: These systems provide a structured approach to incident management, allowing teams to document incidents, assign tasks, and track progress throughout the response lifecycle.

Playbook Automation: Some incident response tools offer automated playbooks that guide responders through predefined response steps based on specific incident types.

This automation helps streamline responses and ensures consistency in handling incidents.

Communication and Collaboration Tools: Effective incident response requires clear communication among team members. Tools such as chat platforms, ticketing systems, and video conferencing solutions enhance collaboration and coordination during incidents.

8. Visualization and Dashboard Tools

Visualization and dashboard tools help threat hunters interpret complex data by presenting it in visually intuitive formats. These tools provide insights into security metrics, trends, and potential threats, enabling informed decision-making.

Customizable Dashboards: Many visualization tools allow organizations to create customizable dashboards that display key metrics, alerts, and visualizations relevant to threat hunting. This customization enhances situational awareness and streamlines monitoring.

Data Analytics and Reporting: Visualization tools often include data analytics capabilities that enable threat hunters to identify patterns and trends over time. Reports generated from these analyses help communicate findings to stakeholders and inform strategic decision-making.

Geolocation and Mapping Features: Some visualization tools incorporate geolocation features, allowing threat hunters to visualize the geographic distribution of threats, attacks, or compromised assets. This capability enhances understanding of potential threat landscapes and targeting.

9. Scripting and Automation Tools

Scripting and automation tools empower threat hunters to automate repetitive tasks, enhance data analysis, and streamline threat-hunting workflows. These tools enable teams to respond to threats more efficiently and reduce the risk of human error.

Scripting Languages: Languages such as Python, PowerShell, and Bash are commonly used for automating tasks, analyzing data, and developing custom tools for specific threat-hunting needs. Skilled hunters can create scripts to extract and analyze data from various sources quickly.

Orchestration Platforms: Security orchestration, automation, and response (SOAR) platforms enable organizations to automate incident response workflows and integrate multiple security tools into a cohesive process. These platforms facilitate collaboration between security teams and improve response times.

Scheduled Tasks and Job Automation: Automation tools can schedule tasks, such as log analysis or data collection, to run at predetermined intervals. This capability ensures that threat-hunting efforts remain consistent and timely.

10. Integrating Tools into the Threat-Hunting Lifecycle

While individual tools play essential roles, the effectiveness of a threat-hunting program relies on the integration of these tools into a cohesive and collaborative workflow. Key considerations for integrating tools include:

Cross-Tool Data Sharing: Ensure that tools can share data seamlessly, allowing for holistic analysis and correlation of findings across the threat-hunting process. Integration between SIEM, EDR, TIPs, and other tools enhances situational awareness.

Automated Workflows: Automate workflows between tools to streamline the threat-hunting process. For example, alerts from a SIEM can trigger automated investigations in EDR tools or prompt data enrichment in a TIP.

Regular Training and Tool Evaluation: Conduct regular training for threat hunters on the capabilities and functionalities of tools. Additionally, evaluate tools periodically to ensure they remain aligned with evolving threats and organizational needs.

The landscape of cyber threats is constantly evolving, and threat hunters must equip themselves with the right tools to effectively detect, analyze, and respond to these threats. From SIEM systems to EDR tools, threat intelligence platforms, and incident response solutions, each tool plays a crucial role in the threat-hunting lifecycle. By leveraging a combination of these core tools and integrating them into a cohesive strategy, organizations can enhance their threat-hunting capabilities, improve incident response times, and ultimately strengthen their overall security posture. As threats continue to become more sophisticated, investing in the right tools will be paramount to successfully navigating the ever-changing threat landscape.

5.2 The Role of Automation and AI

In today's dynamic cyber threat landscape, the scale and sophistication of attacks have increased dramatically, posing significant challenges for cybersecurity teams. To combat these evolving threats, organizations are increasingly turning to automation and artificial intelligence (AI) to enhance their threat-hunting capabilities. This chapter explores how automation and AI are transforming the field of cyber threat hunting, discussing their roles, benefits, applications, and considerations for effective implementation.

1. The Need for Automation in Threat Hunting

As cyber threats become more complex, the volume of data generated within organizations continues to grow exponentially. Security teams are inundated with alerts, logs, and other data that need to be analyzed in real time. This overwhelming amount of information can lead to alert fatigue and delayed response times.

Efficiency in Data Processing: Automation allows organizations to process and analyze vast amounts of security data quickly and accurately. Automated systems can sift through logs, events, and alerts to identify patterns and anomalies, significantly reducing the time threat hunters spend on manual analysis.

Reduction of Human Error: Human analysis is inherently prone to errors, especially when dealing with large volumes of data under pressure. Automation minimizes the risk of human mistakes, ensuring that critical threats are not overlooked due to oversight.

Scalability of Threat-Hunting Efforts: As organizations grow, their security needs become more complex. Automation enables cybersecurity teams to scale their threat-hunting efforts without the need for proportional increases in staffing. This scalability is crucial for maintaining effective security in larger, more distributed environments.

2. The Role of AI in Threat Hunting

AI technologies, particularly machine learning (ML) and deep learning, are playing a pivotal role in advancing threat-hunting efforts. AI enhances the ability to detect, predict, and respond to threats through sophisticated algorithms and data analysis.

Anomaly Detection: AI algorithms can analyze historical data to establish a baseline of normal behavior within an organization. By continuously monitoring for deviations from this baseline, AI can quickly identify anomalies that may indicate a security incident. This proactive approach enables organizations to detect threats before they escalate.

Threat Prediction: Leveraging historical attack patterns and behavioral data, AI can predict potential threats based on emerging trends and adversarial techniques. This predictive capability allows organizations to stay ahead of threat actors and implement preventive measures.

Automated Decision-Making: AI can facilitate automated decision-making processes based on predefined rules and learned behaviors. For instance, when an anomaly is detected, AI can automatically initiate a response protocol, such as isolating a compromised endpoint or blocking suspicious network traffic.

3. Enhancing Threat Intelligence with AI

AI can significantly improve the efficacy of threat intelligence by augmenting data analysis and contextualization.

Data Enrichment: AI algorithms can enhance threat intelligence feeds by correlating indicators of compromise (IOCs) with historical attack data, allowing threat hunters to understand the context of threats better. This enrichment provides valuable insights into threat actors, motives, and TTPs (Tactics, Techniques, and Procedures).

Intelligent Threat Scoring: AI can assign scores to threats based on their potential impact and likelihood, helping security teams prioritize investigations effectively. This prioritization ensures that resources are allocated efficiently to the most critical threats.

Natural Language Processing (NLP): AI-driven NLP technologies can analyze unstructured data, such as threat reports, social media posts, and forums, to extract relevant information about emerging threats. This capability allows threat hunters to tap into a wider range of intelligence sources and gain deeper insights into the threat landscape.

4. Automating Repetitive Tasks in Threat Hunting

Automation can streamline various repetitive tasks in the threat-hunting process, allowing security teams to focus on more strategic activities.

Alert Triage: Automation can assist in triaging alerts generated by SIEM and other monitoring tools. By implementing automated workflows, organizations can filter out false positives and prioritize legitimate threats for further investigation.

Data Collection and Aggregation: Automation tools can continuously collect and aggregate security data from multiple sources, including endpoints, network devices, and threat intelligence feeds. This streamlined data collection ensures that threat hunters have access to comprehensive and up-to-date information.

Automated Reporting: Generating reports on threat-hunting activities, findings, and outcomes can be time-consuming. Automation tools can streamline this process by generating standardized reports, allowing teams to communicate findings to stakeholders efficiently.

5. Machine Learning for Enhanced Detection

Machine learning algorithms can enhance threat detection capabilities by continuously learning from new data and adapting to evolving threats.

Behavioral Analysis: ML models can analyze user and entity behaviors to detect deviations that may signify potential insider threats or compromised accounts. By learning normal patterns, these models can quickly identify anomalies that warrant investigation.

Signature-Free Detection: Traditional signature-based detection methods can be ineffective against new and unknown threats. ML-based detection systems can identify malicious behaviors without relying on predefined signatures, enabling organizations to detect zero-day attacks and novel malware strains.

Continuous Improvement: Machine learning models improve over time as they ingest more data and learn from past incidents. This continuous improvement enhances the accuracy and effectiveness of threat detection efforts.

6. Challenges and Considerations for Automation and AI

While automation and AI offer significant advantages in threat hunting, organizations must also consider several challenges and implications.

Quality of Data: The effectiveness of AI and automation relies heavily on the quality and integrity of the data used for training models. Poor-quality data can lead to inaccurate predictions and detections, potentially resulting in missed threats or false alarms.

Complexity of Implementation: Integrating automation and AI into existing security infrastructure can be complex and resource-intensive. Organizations must assess their current capabilities, invest in the right technologies, and ensure that staff have the necessary skills to leverage these tools effectively.

Over-Reliance on Technology: While automation and AI can enhance threat-hunting efforts, organizations should avoid over-reliance on technology at the expense of human judgment. Cybersecurity remains a human-centric field, and skilled threat hunters play a vital role in interpreting findings, making decisions, and adapting to the evolving threat landscape.

Ethical Considerations: The use of AI in cybersecurity raises ethical concerns related to privacy, bias, and transparency. Organizations must ensure that AI-driven decisions are transparent, fair, and aligned with ethical standards.

7. The Future of Automation and AI in Threat Hunting

The future of threat hunting will likely see increased integration of automation and AI, with organizations continuing to adopt these technologies to enhance their security posture.

Advanced AI Algorithms: As AI technologies evolve, advanced algorithms will enable even more sophisticated detection and response capabilities. Deep learning models may become increasingly adept at recognizing complex attack patterns and predicting future threats.

Greater Collaboration: Automation and AI will facilitate collaboration between security teams and other departments, such as IT and risk management. By integrating threat intelligence across the organization, businesses can strengthen their overall cybersecurity posture.

Evolving Skill Sets: As automation and AI become more prevalent, the skills required for threat hunters will evolve. Cybersecurity professionals will need to develop expertise in AI technologies, data analysis, and automation strategies to leverage these tools effectively.

Automation and AI are revolutionizing the field of cyber threat hunting, enabling organizations to detect, analyze, and respond to threats more efficiently and effectively. By harnessing the power of automation to streamline processes and leveraging AI for advanced detection capabilities, security teams can enhance their threat-hunting efforts and respond proactively to emerging threats. While challenges remain, the potential benefits of these technologies are immense, positioning organizations to better defend against the ever-evolving landscape of cyber threats. As the threat landscape continues to evolve, the integration of automation and AI will become increasingly essential for maintaining effective cybersecurity defenses.

5.3 Comparing Open-Source and Commercial Tools

In the landscape of cyber threat hunting, organizations have a plethora of tools at their disposal, ranging from open-source solutions to commercial products. Each type has its strengths and weaknesses, and the choice between them often depends on various factors, including budget, expertise, organizational needs, and specific use cases. This chapter delves into the comparison between open-source and commercial tools in the context of threat hunting, examining their features, benefits, challenges, and ideal use cases.

1. Overview of Open-Source Tools

Open-source tools are software solutions whose source code is publicly available for anyone to use, modify, and distribute. These tools are often developed collaboratively by communities of users and developers.

Accessibility: Open-source tools are generally free to use, which makes them accessible to a broad audience, including small businesses, educational institutions, and individual researchers. This accessibility allows organizations with limited budgets to implement effective threat-hunting strategies.

Customization and Flexibility: Users can modify open-source tools to fit their specific needs. This flexibility allows organizations to tailor solutions according to their unique environments and threat landscapes. Developers can contribute improvements and new features, enhancing the tool's capabilities over time.

Community Support: Many open-source tools benefit from active communities that provide support, documentation, and resources. Users can access forums, user groups, and online documentation to troubleshoot issues, share experiences, and collaborate on improvements.

2. Overview of Commercial Tools

Commercial tools are proprietary solutions developed and sold by companies. They often come with dedicated support, advanced features, and comprehensive documentation.

Professional Support: Commercial tools typically include access to professional support services, including technical assistance, training, and updates. This support can be invaluable for organizations lacking in-house expertise or resources to troubleshoot issues independently.

Comprehensive Features: Commercial products often come with a wide array of features, including advanced analytics, automation capabilities, and integration with other security solutions. These features can enhance the overall effectiveness of threat-hunting efforts.

User-Friendly Interfaces: Many commercial tools prioritize user experience, providing intuitive interfaces and dashboards that facilitate quick data interpretation and analysis. This ease of use can reduce the learning curve for new users and improve overall efficiency.

3. Cost Considerations

One of the most significant differences between open-source and commercial tools lies in their cost structures.

Open-Source Cost Benefits: Open-source tools are often free to use, which can provide substantial savings for organizations. However, there may still be indirect costs associated with implementing these tools, such as the need for skilled personnel to manage and maintain the systems, as well as potential costs related to custom development or integration with existing infrastructure.

Commercial Licensing Fees: Commercial tools typically require licensing fees, which can vary widely depending on the vendor, the features included, and the size of the organization. While these tools may involve higher upfront costs, they often provide value through enhanced support, training, and continuous updates.

Total Cost of Ownership (TCO): When evaluating costs, organizations should consider the total cost of ownership, including initial investments, ongoing maintenance, training, and operational expenses. Open-source tools may appear cheaper initially, but long-term costs can accumulate based on the resources needed for effective management.

4. Ease of Implementation and Use

The ease of implementation and use is crucial for organizations seeking to deploy threat-hunting tools quickly and effectively.

Open-Source Complexity: Open-source tools can require significant technical expertise to implement and customize effectively. Organizations may need to allocate resources for installation, configuration, and ongoing maintenance, which can lead to longer deployment times.

Commercial Tools and Quick Setup: Many commercial solutions offer streamlined installation processes, allowing organizations to deploy them quickly and start using them with minimal disruption. Vendors often provide onboarding assistance and training, further simplifying implementation.

Learning Curve: The learning curve for open-source tools can vary based on the complexity of the tool and the availability of documentation and community resources. Commercial tools often provide comprehensive documentation and training resources, making them easier to learn for users who may be less experienced in threat hunting.

5. Features and Functionality

The features and functionality offered by open-source and commercial tools can vary significantly, impacting their effectiveness for threat hunting.

Open-Source Feature Range: Open-source tools may not always offer the comprehensive features found in commercial products. While many open-source tools are highly capable, some may lack advanced analytics, reporting capabilities, or integration with other security solutions. However, the flexibility of open-source tools allows users to develop custom features to meet their needs.

Commercial Tool Robustness: Commercial tools often come with robust features, including advanced threat detection algorithms, real-time monitoring, and automated reporting. These features can enhance threat-hunting capabilities and provide deeper insights into potential threats.

Integration Capabilities: Commercial solutions typically prioritize integration with other security products, such as SIEM systems, EDR tools, and threat intelligence platforms. This integration facilitates a more cohesive security posture. Open-source tools can also integrate with other systems, but organizations may need to invest additional resources in developing and managing these integrations.

6. Security and Updates

Security is paramount in threat hunting, and how tools are maintained and updated can affect their effectiveness.

Open-Source Vulnerability Management: Open-source tools rely on the community for updates and security patches. While this model can lead to rapid improvements and innovations, it may also result in delayed responses to vulnerabilities. Organizations must be proactive in monitoring and applying updates.

Commercial Vendor Responsibility: Commercial vendors have a vested interest in maintaining the security of their products. They typically provide regular updates, patches, and support to address vulnerabilities quickly. This proactive approach can offer organizations peace of mind regarding the security of their tools.

7. Ideal Use Cases

Understanding the ideal use cases for open-source and commercial tools can help organizations make informed decisions based on their specific needs and capabilities.

Open-Source Ideal Use Cases: Open-source tools are well-suited for small to medium-sized organizations, research institutions, and teams with strong technical expertise. They can also be beneficial for organizations looking to customize their tools or those with limited budgets. Additionally, open-source solutions can be used for experimental purposes or in educational settings.

Commercial Ideal Use Cases: Commercial tools are often the best choice for large enterprises, organizations with extensive regulatory requirements, or those lacking in-house cybersecurity expertise. They provide comprehensive support, features, and integrations that are critical for complex environments. Organizations that prioritize rapid deployment and ease of use may also benefit from commercial solutions.

The choice between open-source and commercial tools for threat hunting ultimately depends on an organization's specific needs, budget, and technical capabilities. Open-source tools offer flexibility, cost-effectiveness, and community support, making them attractive for organizations with strong technical teams. In contrast, commercial tools provide comprehensive features, professional support, and ease of use, making them ideal for organizations seeking robust solutions and rapid deployment.

To maximize the effectiveness of threat-hunting efforts, organizations may also consider a hybrid approach, utilizing both open-source and commercial tools in conjunction to leverage the strengths of each. By carefully evaluating their needs and conducting thorough research, organizations can select the tools that best align with their threat-hunting objectives and enhance their overall cybersecurity posture. As the threat landscape continues to evolve, the right tools will be critical for staying ahead of emerging threats and effectively safeguarding organizational assets.

6. The Threat Hunting Process: From Hypothesis to Investigation

The threat hunting process is a systematic approach that transforms intelligence and intuition into actionable insights, enabling security teams to detect threats before they can cause harm. In this chapter, we will outline the key steps in the threat hunting lifecycle, beginning with hypothesis formulation—where hunters create educated assumptions based on threat intelligence and observed anomalies. We will discuss the importance of effective data collection, highlighting the critical data sources and types of information needed to support the investigation. As we progress through the investigation phase, we will cover analytical techniques and methodologies that help hunters identify indicators of compromise and uncover hidden threats. By understanding and mastering the threat hunting process from hypothesis to investigation, organizations can develop a proactive stance against cyber threats, improving their detection capabilities and overall resilience in the face of emerging risks.

6.1 Building and Testing Hypotheses

In the realm of cyber threat hunting, building and testing hypotheses is a fundamental process that allows security professionals to proactively identify and investigate potential threats within their environments. Rather than merely reacting to alerts generated by automated systems, threat hunters take a more analytical approach, formulating educated guesses about possible security incidents based on known patterns and behaviors. This chapter explores the importance of hypothesis-driven hunting, the steps involved in building and testing hypotheses, and best practices for successful implementation.

1. The Importance of Hypothesis-Driven Hunting

Hypothesis-driven hunting shifts the focus from reactive incident response to a proactive exploration of the environment, enabling organizations to uncover hidden threats and vulnerabilities.

Proactive Threat Detection: By formulating hypotheses about potential threats, hunters can actively seek out indicators of compromise (IOCs) and anomalous behaviors that might otherwise go unnoticed. This proactive approach allows organizations to detect and respond to threats before they escalate into significant incidents.

Efficient Resource Allocation: Instead of pursuing every alert or potential threat indiscriminately, hypothesis-driven hunting enables teams to focus their efforts on the most relevant areas of concern. By prioritizing investigations based on specific hypotheses, organizations can use their resources more effectively.

Enhanced Understanding of the Environment: Building and testing hypotheses fosters a deeper understanding of the organization's unique threat landscape. Threat hunters gain insights into the behavior of users, applications, and systems, helping them to identify patterns and anomalies that may indicate malicious activity.

2. Steps in Building a Hypothesis

Building a hypothesis involves a systematic approach that draws on existing knowledge, data analysis, and an understanding of the threat landscape. Here are the key steps involved:

2.1 Identifying the Focus Area

The first step in building a hypothesis is identifying the specific area of concern within the organization's environment. This could be based on recent security incidents, trends in threat intelligence, or particular vulnerabilities that need to be addressed.

Data Sources: Analyze data from various sources, including logs, alerts, threat intelligence feeds, and user behavior analytics, to identify potential patterns or anomalies.

Business Context: Consider the organization's business context, such as its industry, regulatory requirements, and recent changes in operations that might affect its threat landscape.

2.2 Gathering Contextual Information

Once a focus area has been identified, the next step is to gather relevant contextual information that will inform the hypothesis.

Threat Intelligence: Utilize threat intelligence to understand common tactics, techniques, and procedures (TTPs) employed by adversaries targeting similar organizations. This knowledge can provide valuable insights into potential attack vectors and motivations.

Historical Data: Review historical data related to past incidents and known vulnerabilities. Understanding how previous threats manifested can help shape the current hypothesis.

2.3 Formulating the Hypothesis

With contextual information in hand, the next step is to formulate a clear and concise hypothesis that can be tested.

Clarity and Specificity: A good hypothesis should be clear, specific, and testable. For example, "Malicious actors are exploiting unpatched vulnerabilities in the web application" is a specific hypothesis that can be investigated.

Defining Indicators of Compromise (IOCs): Identify specific IOCs or behaviors that would support or refute the hypothesis. These could include unusual login attempts, unauthorized access to sensitive data, or traffic patterns associated with known malware.

3. Testing the Hypothesis

Once a hypothesis has been formulated, it must be tested to determine its validity. This process involves data collection, analysis, and interpretation.

3.1 Data Collection

Collect relevant data that can help verify or disprove the hypothesis.

Log Analysis: Review system and application logs, network traffic data, and user activity logs to identify evidence supporting the hypothesis.

Threat Hunting Tools: Utilize threat-hunting tools and technologies to automate data collection and analysis. Tools that provide query capabilities across large data sets can be particularly effective in identifying patterns.

3.2 Analysis and Interpretation

Once data has been collected, it must be analyzed to draw conclusions about the hypothesis.

Data Correlation: Correlate the collected data with the IOCs defined in the hypothesis. Look for signs of malicious activity that align with the predictions made in the hypothesis.

Anomaly Detection: Identify any deviations from expected behavior. If the hypothesis posits that specific actions or patterns should not occur under normal circumstances, look for evidence of those anomalies in the data.

3.3 Validation or Refinement

Based on the analysis, determine whether the hypothesis is supported or refuted.

Supporting Evidence: If the data supports the hypothesis, document the findings and consider the implications for the organization's security posture. This may involve escalating the findings for further investigation or remediation.

Refinement: If the hypothesis is not supported, analyze why it failed. This process of refinement is crucial for improving future hypotheses and hunting efforts. Consider whether the initial assumptions were flawed, if additional context is needed, or if new IOCs should be established.

4. Best Practices for Building and Testing Hypotheses

To enhance the effectiveness of hypothesis-driven threat hunting, organizations should consider the following best practices:

4.1 Collaboration and Knowledge Sharing

Encourage collaboration among team members and knowledge sharing across departments. Engaging with other security professionals, threat intelligence analysts, and incident response teams can provide valuable insights and diverse perspectives on potential threats.

4.2 Iterative Process

Recognize that hypothesis-driven hunting is an iterative process. As new threats emerge and the environment evolves, continuously refine and adjust hypotheses based on the latest information and insights.

4.3 Documentation

Thoroughly document the hypotheses, findings, and lessons learned throughout the process. Documentation not only provides a record of the threat-hunting efforts but also facilitates knowledge transfer and future improvements.

4.4 Continuous Learning

Promote a culture of continuous learning within the threat-hunting team. Encourage team members to stay updated on the latest threat intelligence, industry trends, and emerging technologies that may impact the organization's security posture.

Building and testing hypotheses is a cornerstone of effective cyber threat hunting. By adopting a systematic approach that emphasizes proactive investigation, organizations can uncover hidden threats and vulnerabilities before they lead to significant incidents. Through careful formulation and testing of hypotheses, security teams can enhance their understanding of the threat landscape, improve their detection capabilities, and ultimately strengthen their cybersecurity posture. As the threat landscape continues to evolve, organizations that embrace hypothesis-driven hunting will be better equipped to anticipate and respond to emerging threats, ensuring a more resilient security environment.

6.2 Data Collection Essentials

In the realm of cyber threat hunting, data collection is a critical component that underpins the entire investigative process. The effectiveness of threat hunting efforts hinges on the quality and comprehensiveness of the data collected, as it forms the foundation for analysis, hypothesis testing, and ultimately, decision-making. This chapter delves into the essentials of data collection in cyber threat hunting, covering key data sources, collection methods, best practices, and the importance of data quality.

1. Understanding Data Types

Data in the context of cyber threat hunting can be broadly categorized into several types, each providing unique insights into the security landscape.

1.1 Log Data

Log data is one of the primary sources of information for threat hunters. It includes records generated by systems, applications, and network devices, capturing events and transactions that occur within the environment.

System Logs: These logs capture events occurring at the operating system level, such as user logins, file access, and system errors. They can provide valuable information about user activities and system behavior.

Application Logs: Application logs record events specific to software applications, including errors, transactions, and user interactions. Analyzing these logs can help identify abnormal application behavior that may indicate a compromise.

Network Logs: Network logs capture information about traffic flowing through the network, including connection attempts, data transfers, and communications between devices. This data is crucial for identifying malicious traffic patterns and unauthorized access attempts.

1.2 Threat Intelligence Data

Threat intelligence data provides context about potential threats, vulnerabilities, and adversary behaviors. This data can be sourced from various external and internal channels.

External Intelligence Feeds: Organizations can subscribe to threat intelligence feeds that provide timely information about emerging threats, malware signatures, and TTPs used by adversaries.

Internal Intelligence: Internal threat intelligence is gathered from previous incidents, vulnerabilities discovered during assessments, and patterns identified through monitoring. This data is vital for understanding the specific threats facing the organization.

1.3 User Behavior Data

User behavior data captures patterns of how individuals interact with systems and applications. Analyzing this data helps identify anomalies that may indicate insider threats or compromised accounts.

User Activity Logs: These logs record user activities, including login times, access patterns, and actions taken within applications. Deviations from established patterns may signal potential malicious behavior.

Behavioral Analytics: Tools that leverage machine learning and statistical analysis can identify unusual user behaviors, providing alerts for further investigation.

2. Key Data Sources for Threat Hunting

To effectively collect data for threat hunting, organizations must identify and leverage various key data sources.

2.1 Endpoint Data

Endpoints, including workstations, servers, and mobile devices, generate a wealth of data that can provide insights into user activities and potential threats.

Endpoint Detection and Response (EDR): EDR solutions monitor endpoint activities and provide detailed visibility into processes, file changes, and network connections. They are essential for identifying indicators of compromise on individual devices.

Sysmon: Sysinternals Sysmon is a tool that provides advanced logging capabilities for Windows systems. It captures detailed information about process creations, network connections, and changes to files, offering valuable data for threat hunters.

2.2 Network Data

Network data offers insights into traffic patterns, communications between devices, and potential unauthorized access attempts.

Network Traffic Analysis: Tools that analyze network traffic can provide visibility into data flows, helping identify anomalies such as unusual communication patterns, unexpected data transfers, or connections to known malicious IP addresses.

Firewall and IDS/IPS Logs: Firewalls and intrusion detection/prevention systems generate logs that capture traffic that is allowed or blocked based on established rules. Analyzing these logs can reveal potential threats attempting to breach the network perimeter.

2.3 Cloud and Application Data

As organizations increasingly migrate to cloud environments and use various applications, collecting data from these sources is crucial.

Cloud Service Logs: Cloud service providers often offer logging capabilities that track user activities, API calls, and access attempts. Collecting this data is essential for monitoring and securing cloud-based resources.

Application Performance Monitoring (APM): APM tools provide insights into application behavior, including performance metrics, user interactions, and error rates. Monitoring these metrics can help identify potential application vulnerabilities or malicious activities.

3. Data Collection Methods

Once the key data sources have been identified, organizations must implement effective data collection methods to gather the necessary information.

3.1 Centralized Logging Solutions

Centralized logging solutions aggregate log data from various sources into a single location for analysis and monitoring.

Security Information and Event Management (SIEM): SIEM solutions collect, analyze, and correlate log data from multiple sources in real-time. They provide dashboards and alerts that help security teams identify potential threats quickly.

Log Management Systems: Dedicated log management tools can help organizations collect, store, and analyze logs from various devices and applications. These systems facilitate long-term storage and enable efficient searches for specific events.

3.2 Data Enrichment

Enriching collected data with additional context can enhance its value for threat hunting.

Threat Intelligence Integration: Integrating threat intelligence data with collected logs allows hunters to correlate observed behaviors with known threats, providing deeper insights into potential malicious activities.

User Context: Augmenting user behavior data with contextual information (e.g., role, location, and previous behavior) can help security teams better understand anomalies and assess the likelihood of malicious intent.

3.3 Automation and Scripting

Automation plays a vital role in efficient data collection and analysis.

Automated Collection Scripts: Organizations can develop scripts that automate the collection of logs and data from various sources, reducing the burden on security teams and ensuring consistency.

Scheduled Data Pulls: Regularly scheduled data pulls from various sources ensure that threat hunters have access to up-to-date information, facilitating timely investigations.

4. Ensuring Data Quality

Data quality is critical for effective threat hunting. High-quality data leads to accurate analysis and informed decision-making.

4.1 Completeness

Ensure that all relevant data sources are included in the data collection process. Incomplete data can lead to blind spots in threat detection and analysis.

4.2 Accuracy

Data accuracy is essential for reliable threat hunting. Regularly verify and validate collected data to identify and correct inaccuracies.

4.3 Timeliness

Timely data collection is vital for effective threat hunting. Delays in data collection can hinder the ability to respond to incidents swiftly. Implement real-time or near-real-time data collection processes whenever possible.

4.4 Consistency

Consistent data formatting and collection methods across different sources simplify analysis and enable better correlation of events.

Data collection is a cornerstone of effective cyber threat hunting. By understanding the various types of data available, identifying key data sources, and implementing efficient collection methods, organizations can build a robust foundation for their threat-hunting efforts. Emphasizing data quality ensures that threat hunters can analyze accurate, complete, and timely information, leading to more effective threat detection and response. As the threat landscape continues to evolve, organizations that prioritize data collection essentials will be better equipped to identify and mitigate potential threats, enhancing their overall cybersecurity posture.

6.3 Investigative Techniques and Analysis

In the field of cyber threat hunting, effective investigative techniques and analysis are essential for identifying and mitigating potential threats. Once data is collected, threat hunters must employ a variety of analytical methods to sift through the information, drawing meaningful insights and identifying anomalies that may indicate malicious activity. This chapter explores several key investigative techniques, analytical methods, and the importance of a systematic approach to threat hunting.

1. The Role of Investigative Techniques

Investigative techniques in threat hunting serve to uncover hidden threats and vulnerabilities within an organization's environment. By applying systematic methods to data analysis, hunters can identify patterns, correlations, and anomalies that might otherwise go unnoticed.

1.1 Anomaly Detection

Anomaly detection involves identifying deviations from normal behavior patterns. This technique is crucial in threat hunting, as many cyber threats manifest as unusual activities that can be detected if a baseline of normal behavior is established.

Baseline Behavior: Establishing a baseline of normal activity is fundamental for effective anomaly detection. This may involve monitoring user behaviors, network traffic patterns, and system performance metrics over time to understand what constitutes "normal."

Statistical Analysis: Statistical methods can be employed to determine the significance of deviations from established norms. For instance, standard deviation and z-scores can help quantify how far an event strays from expected behavior.

1.2 Pattern Recognition

Pattern recognition involves identifying recurring patterns or trends in data that may signify malicious activity. This technique leverages machine learning and data mining techniques to automate the detection of known threats.

Machine Learning Models: By training machine learning algorithms on historical data, hunters can develop models that recognize patterns associated with specific types of attacks, such as lateral movement or data exfiltration.

Behavioral Indicators: Identifying behavioral indicators of compromise (IoCs) allows hunters to proactively search for signs of potential threats. These indicators can include unusual file access patterns, unexpected logins, or anomalous network traffic.

1.3 Correlation Analysis

Correlation analysis involves examining relationships between different data points to identify potential threats. This technique is particularly useful for connecting seemingly unrelated events to reveal broader security issues.

Cross-Data Source Correlation: Threat hunters should correlate data from multiple sources, such as logs, threat intelligence feeds, and user behavior data. This holistic view can help uncover complex attack patterns that might not be evident when analyzing individual data sources in isolation.

Temporal Correlation: Analyzing events in the context of time can reveal significant relationships. For example, a sudden increase in failed login attempts followed by successful logins may indicate an ongoing brute-force attack.

2. Analytical Methods for Threat Hunting

A variety of analytical methods can be employed to support investigative techniques in threat hunting. Each method serves a different purpose and can provide unique insights into potential threats.

2.1 Hypothesis Testing

Building on the foundation of hypothesis-driven hunting, hypothesis testing is a structured analytical method that involves formulating hypotheses based on known threat indicators and then testing them against collected data.

Formulating Hypotheses: Threat hunters should develop specific, testable hypotheses about potential threats. For instance, a hypothesis might state that "unusual login attempts from a specific geographic region indicate credential theft."

Testing and Validating: By analyzing the collected data against the hypothesis, hunters can either validate or refute their initial assumptions. If validated, the findings can prompt further investigation or immediate response measures.

2.2 Time Series Analysis

Time series analysis is a technique used to analyze data points collected over time. This method is particularly effective for identifying trends and patterns in network traffic, user behavior, and system performance.

Trend Analysis: By examining trends in data over time, hunters can identify anomalies that may signify emerging threats. For example, a steady increase in data transfers during off-hours may indicate unauthorized data exfiltration.

Event Sequence Analysis: Time series data allows hunters to analyze the sequence of events leading up to a potential incident. Understanding the timeline of activities can provide critical insights into attack progression and methods employed by adversaries.

2.3 Forensic Analysis

Forensic analysis involves a deep dive into specific incidents to uncover details about how they occurred, what systems were affected, and what data may have been compromised.

File and Artifact Analysis: Investigating file changes, creation times, and metadata can reveal critical information about malicious activities. Analyzing artifacts left behind by attackers, such as malware remnants or suspicious files, can provide insights into their methods.

Memory Forensics: Memory analysis tools can extract and analyze the contents of a system's memory to identify running processes, network connections, and other artifacts that may indicate an ongoing compromise.

3. Utilizing Threat Hunting Tools

Effective investigative techniques are often supported by specialized threat hunting tools that streamline data analysis and enhance the hunting process.

3.1 Security Information and Event Management (SIEM)

SIEM platforms are essential tools for aggregating and analyzing log data from multiple sources. They enable threat hunters to monitor events in real time and correlate alerts with known threats.

Event Correlation and Analysis: SIEM systems can automatically correlate events from different data sources, allowing hunters to quickly identify patterns and potential threats.

Dashboards and Reporting: SIEM tools often provide customizable dashboards that help visualize data trends and anomalies, making it easier for hunters to spot potential issues.

3.2 Endpoint Detection and Response (EDR)

EDR solutions focus on monitoring endpoints for suspicious activities, offering detailed visibility into processes, file changes, and user actions.

Real-time Monitoring: EDR tools provide continuous monitoring of endpoints, allowing hunters to detect threats as they occur and respond swiftly to potential incidents.

Automated Threat Detection: Many EDR solutions utilize machine learning algorithms to detect unusual behaviors and patterns on endpoints, streamlining the threat detection process.

3.3 Threat Intelligence Platforms

Threat intelligence platforms aggregate and analyze threat data from various sources, providing valuable context for threat hunters.

Contextual Insights: By integrating threat intelligence with collected data, hunters can better understand the relevance of specific indicators and prioritize their investigations accordingly.

Automated Threat Correlation: These platforms often include capabilities for automatically correlating observed behaviors with known threats, facilitating faster detection of potential incidents.

4. Best Practices for Investigative Analysis

To enhance the effectiveness of investigative techniques and analysis in threat hunting, organizations should adhere to several best practices:

4.1 Maintain a Clear Focus

During investigations, it is essential to maintain a clear focus on specific hypotheses or areas of concern. Avoiding unnecessary distractions ensures that threat hunters can efficiently allocate their resources and time.

4.2 Document Findings and Insights

Thorough documentation of investigative processes, findings, and insights is vital for continuous improvement. Maintaining clear records helps facilitate knowledge transfer, informs future investigations, and contributes to organizational learning.

4.3 Collaborate Across Teams

Encouraging collaboration among threat hunting teams, incident response teams, and threat intelligence analysts fosters knowledge sharing and diverse perspectives, ultimately enhancing the effectiveness of investigations.

4.4 Continuous Improvement

Threat hunting is an evolving field, and organizations must prioritize continuous improvement. Regularly review and refine investigative techniques based on lessons learned, emerging threats, and advances in technology.

Investigative techniques and analysis are fundamental components of effective cyber threat hunting. By employing various methods such as anomaly detection, pattern recognition, correlation analysis, and hypothesis testing, threat hunters can uncover hidden threats and vulnerabilities within their environments. Utilizing advanced tools and adhering to best practices further enhances the effectiveness of investigative efforts. As the cyber threat landscape continues to evolve, organizations that prioritize robust investigative techniques will be better equipped to identify, respond to, and mitigate potential threats, ensuring a stronger overall security posture.

7. Behavioral Analysis and Anomaly Detection

Behavioral analysis and anomaly detection are pivotal components of effective threat hunting, enabling security teams to identify suspicious activities that deviate from established norms. In this chapter, we will explore the principles of behavior-based detection, emphasizing how understanding user and entity behavior can reveal potential security threats. We will discuss techniques for establishing baseline behaviors, which serve as reference points for identifying anomalies indicative of malicious activity. Additionally, we will delve into various anomaly detection methods, including statistical analysis, machine learning algorithms, and heuristics, detailing how they can be leveraged to enhance threat detection capabilities. By honing in on behavioral patterns and recognizing anomalies, organizations can significantly improve their chances of detecting and mitigating cyber threats before they escalate, fostering a proactive and resilient cybersecurity environment.

7.1 Understanding Behavior-Based Detection

In the realm of cyber threat hunting, behavior-based detection has emerged as a critical approach for identifying and mitigating sophisticated cyber threats. Unlike traditional signature-based detection methods, which rely on known patterns or signatures of malicious activity, behavior-based detection focuses on analyzing the behavior of users, applications, and systems to identify anomalies that may signify a potential compromise. This chapter explores the principles of behavior-based detection, its advantages over traditional methods, and its implementation within threat hunting programs.

1. The Foundations of Behavior-Based Detection

Behavior-based detection is grounded in the understanding that malicious activities often exhibit unique behavioral patterns that can be detected, even if the specific attack signature is unknown. This approach allows security teams to identify threats that may bypass signature-based systems, providing a more proactive means of threat detection.

1.1 Defining Behavior-Based Detection

At its core, behavior-based detection involves the continuous monitoring and analysis of system and user behaviors to identify deviations from established norms. These deviations can indicate potentially malicious activities, such as unauthorized access attempts, data exfiltration, or lateral movement within a network.

User Behavior Analytics (UBA): UBA is a subset of behavior-based detection that specifically focuses on monitoring user actions and identifying unusual behavior patterns. For example, if an employee who typically accesses files during business hours suddenly attempts to access sensitive data at odd hours, this may trigger an alert for further investigation.

Entity Behavior Analytics (EBA): Similar to UBA, EBA expands the focus to include the behavior of entities within the network, such as servers, applications, and devices. This approach helps identify anomalies in system behavior that could indicate compromise or exploitation.

1.2 Establishing a Baseline

For behavior-based detection to be effective, organizations must establish a baseline of normal behavior for users and systems. This baseline serves as a reference point for identifying anomalies.

Data Collection: Continuous monitoring and collection of data are essential for establishing a comprehensive baseline. This may include logs from various sources, such as endpoints, applications, and network devices.

Behavior Modeling: By analyzing historical data, organizations can model normal behavior patterns for users and systems. Machine learning algorithms can be employed to create models that adapt over time as behavior changes.

2. Advantages of Behavior-Based Detection

Behavior-based detection offers several advantages over traditional signature-based methods, making it a valuable addition to any threat hunting program.

2.1 Proactive Threat Detection

One of the primary benefits of behavior-based detection is its proactive nature. By focusing on behavioral anomalies rather than known signatures, organizations can identify threats before they manifest into full-blown incidents.

Zero-Day Threat Detection: Behavior-based detection is particularly effective against zero-day vulnerabilities and advanced persistent threats (APTs) that may not have known signatures. By monitoring for unusual behaviors, security teams can detect these threats in real time.

Insider Threat Detection: Insider threats often evade traditional detection methods because they utilize legitimate access to exploit systems. Behavior-based detection helps identify unusual actions taken by insiders, enabling organizations to respond before significant damage occurs.

2.2 Reduced False Positives

Traditional signature-based detection systems often generate a high volume of false positives, leading to alert fatigue and reduced efficiency for security teams. Behavior-based detection can help mitigate this issue.

Contextual Analysis: Behavior-based detection systems analyze the context of actions taken by users and systems. This context allows security teams to differentiate between benign anomalies and potential threats, reducing the overall number of false alerts.

Adaptive Learning: Many behavior-based detection systems leverage machine learning to adapt to changing environments. As user behaviors evolve, these systems can recalibrate their baseline models, improving accuracy and reducing false positives over time.

2.3 Comprehensive Visibility

Behavior-based detection provides organizations with a more comprehensive view of their security posture. By monitoring behaviors across users, applications, and systems, security teams can identify interconnected anomalies that may indicate complex attack scenarios.

Holistic Monitoring: Rather than focusing solely on known signatures, behavior-based detection enables a more holistic approach to security monitoring. This visibility allows organizations to identify multi-faceted threats and respond more effectively.

Correlation of Events: Behavior-based detection systems can correlate events across different data sources, providing deeper insights into potential threats. For example, if multiple users exhibit unusual behaviors simultaneously, this may indicate coordinated malicious activity.

3. Implementation of Behavior-Based Detection

To effectively implement behavior-based detection within a threat hunting program, organizations must follow a systematic approach.

3.1 Data Sources and Integration

The first step in implementing behavior-based detection is identifying and integrating relevant data sources.

Log Collection: Organizations should gather logs from endpoints, servers, applications, and network devices to provide a comprehensive view of activities. SIEM solutions can facilitate the aggregation of this data for analysis.

Threat Intelligence Integration: Integrating threat intelligence feeds can enhance the context of behavioral analysis. This additional data helps security teams understand the potential relevance of observed anomalies.

3.2 Behavior Modeling and Analysis

Once data is collected, organizations can model and analyze user and system behaviors to identify anomalies.

Baseline Creation: By analyzing historical data, organizations can establish baselines for normal behaviors. Machine learning algorithms can assist in developing adaptive models that evolve as behavior changes.

Anomaly Detection Algorithms: Employing various anomaly detection algorithms, such as clustering, statistical analysis, or supervised learning, enables security teams to identify deviations from established baselines effectively.

3.3 Continuous Monitoring and Response

Behavior-based detection is not a one-time effort; it requires continuous monitoring and an iterative approach to threat hunting.

Real-time Monitoring: Organizations should implement real-time monitoring capabilities to detect anomalies as they occur. This enables rapid response to potential threats before they escalate.

Incident Response Planning: Establishing a clear incident response plan is essential for effective mitigation of identified threats. Security teams should have predefined protocols for investigating anomalies and responding to potential incidents.

4. Challenges and Considerations

While behavior-based detection offers significant advantages, organizations must also be aware of its challenges.

4.1 Complexity of Implementation

Implementing behavior-based detection can be complex, requiring a robust understanding of user and system behaviors, as well as the integration of various data sources. Organizations must invest in the right tools, technologies, and expertise to ensure successful deployment.

4.2 Privacy Concerns

Monitoring user behaviors raises privacy concerns that organizations must address. It is crucial to implement behavior-based detection in compliance with relevant regulations and to ensure that user data is handled responsibly.

4.3 Evolving Threat Landscape

As cyber threats continue to evolve, behavior-based detection systems must adapt accordingly. Organizations should regularly review and update their detection models to account for new tactics, techniques, and procedures (TTPs) used by adversaries.

Behavior-based detection is a powerful approach for identifying and mitigating cyber threats in an increasingly complex and dynamic environment. By focusing on the analysis of user and system behaviors, organizations can proactively detect anomalies that may signify potential compromises, reducing the likelihood of successful attacks. Implementing behavior-based detection requires a systematic approach, including data collection, behavior modeling, and continuous monitoring. As the cyber threat landscape evolves, organizations that embrace behavior-based detection will be better equipped to defend against sophisticated threats, ensuring a stronger overall security posture.

7.2 Establishing Normal vs. Abnormal Behaviors

In the world of cybersecurity, differentiating between normal and abnormal behaviors is a fundamental aspect of effective threat detection and response. Understanding what constitutes "normal" behavior for users, applications, and systems is crucial for identifying anomalies that may indicate malicious activity. This chapter delves into the processes and methodologies involved in establishing these baselines, the techniques for recognizing abnormal behaviors, and the implications for threat hunting efforts.

1. The Importance of Establishing Baselines

Establishing a baseline of normal behavior is essential for effective behavior-based detection. This baseline serves as a reference point against which deviations can be measured. Without a clear understanding of what is considered normal, it becomes challenging to identify anomalies that may signify potential threats.

1.1 Defining Normal Behavior

Normal behavior refers to the expected patterns of activity for users, applications, and systems within an organization. This may encompass various aspects, including:

User Behavior: Typical actions performed by users, such as login times, access to specific files or applications, and frequency of data transfers.

System Activity: Regular operations of systems and applications, including CPU usage, memory consumption, and network traffic patterns.

Application Behavior: The expected performance and usage patterns of applications, including response times and data request volumes.

Establishing these norms requires careful observation and data collection over time.

1.2 Data Collection for Baseline Establishment

To effectively define normal behavior, organizations must collect relevant data from various sources:

Log Files: Collecting logs from endpoints, servers, firewalls, and applications provides insight into user and system activities. These logs serve as a foundational dataset for establishing behavioral baselines.

Network Traffic Monitoring: Analyzing network traffic patterns can reveal typical data flows, such as communication between specific servers and users or regular access to external resources.

User Activity Monitoring: Tracking user actions, such as logins, file access, and application usage, helps identify typical behavior patterns.

Historical Data Analysis: Leveraging historical data allows organizations to recognize trends and patterns in behavior over time, contributing to the development of a comprehensive baseline.

2. Techniques for Establishing Normal vs. Abnormal Behaviors

Once relevant data has been collected, various techniques can be employed to establish normal behaviors and identify deviations.

2.1 Statistical Analysis

Statistical methods are often employed to analyze data and establish baselines for normal behavior.

Descriptive Statistics: Basic statistical measures, such as mean, median, mode, and standard deviation, help identify central tendencies and variability in user or system behavior. For example, if most users log in between 8 AM and 6 PM, any login attempts outside this window may be considered abnormal.

Control Charts: Control charts visualize data over time, allowing organizations to monitor behavior against established control limits. If data points fall outside these limits, they may indicate abnormal behavior.

2.2 Machine Learning Techniques

Machine learning offers advanced methods for establishing normal behavior baselines and detecting anomalies.

Supervised Learning: In this approach, models are trained using labeled datasets that distinguish between normal and abnormal behaviors. For instance, historical data can be used to train a model to recognize typical user behaviors.

Unsupervised Learning: Unlike supervised learning, unsupervised learning does not rely on labeled data. Instead, algorithms cluster data points based on similarities, enabling the identification of outliers or abnormal behaviors without predefined labels.

Anomaly Detection Algorithms: Techniques such as clustering, decision trees, and neural networks can be utilized to identify patterns and detect deviations from established norms.

2.3 Behavioral Profiling

Behavioral profiling involves creating detailed profiles of user and system behaviors based on collected data.

User Profiles: For each user, organizations can develop profiles that outline their typical behaviors, such as login patterns, resource usage, and interaction with applications. Any significant deviations from these profiles may trigger alerts for further investigation.

System Profiles: Similarly, system profiles can be created to define normal operational behaviors. Anomalies in resource consumption, application performance, or network traffic can indicate potential threats.

3. Recognizing Abnormal Behaviors

Once normal behaviors have been established, the next step is recognizing abnormal behaviors that may indicate potential security incidents.

3.1 Types of Abnormal Behaviors

Abnormal behaviors can manifest in various forms and may include:

Unusual Login Patterns: Logins from unexpected geographic locations, multiple failed login attempts, or logins during unusual hours can indicate credential theft or brute-force attacks.

Data Access Anomalies: Unexplained access to sensitive files or data by users who typically do not engage with those resources can signal insider threats or compromised accounts.

Resource Consumption Spikes: Sudden spikes in CPU or memory usage, unexpected network traffic patterns, or abnormal application behavior can indicate malware infections or data exfiltration attempts.

3.2 Alerting and Investigation

Once abnormal behaviors are detected, organizations should have processes in place for alerting security teams and conducting investigations.

Alerting Mechanisms: Security information and event management (SIEM) systems can automatically generate alerts based on predefined thresholds for abnormal behaviors, ensuring that security teams are promptly notified.

Investigation Protocols: When an alert is triggered, security teams should follow established investigation protocols to analyze the context of the abnormal behavior, determine its severity, and initiate appropriate response actions.

4. Challenges in Establishing Normal vs. Abnormal Behaviors

While establishing normal versus abnormal behaviors is crucial for effective threat detection, several challenges can arise:

4.1 Dynamic Environments

Organizations today operate in dynamic environments where user behaviors and system configurations can change frequently. This can complicate the process of establishing stable baselines.

Continuous Adaptation: Organizations must ensure that their baseline models can adapt to evolving behaviors, incorporating new data to refine their understanding of normal activities.

4.2 Insider Threats

Insider threats can be particularly challenging to detect because malicious insiders may exploit their legitimate access to carry out harmful activities.

Behavioral Camouflage: Malicious insiders may attempt to mimic normal behaviors to evade detection, making it difficult to distinguish between legitimate actions and malicious intent.

4.3 Volume of Data

The sheer volume of data generated by user and system activities can overwhelm security teams and tools, making it challenging to analyze and establish accurate baselines.

Automation and Tools: To address this challenge, organizations should leverage automation and advanced analytics tools to process large datasets and identify patterns more efficiently.

Establishing a clear distinction between normal and abnormal behaviors is a foundational element of effective threat hunting and behavior-based detection. By defining normal behavior through data collection, statistical analysis, and machine learning techniques, organizations can proactively identify anomalies that may indicate potential threats. However, challenges such as dynamic environments and insider threats necessitate continuous adaptation and the use of advanced tools for effective monitoring and detection. Ultimately, organizations that prioritize the establishment of clear behavioral baselines will be better positioned to defend against emerging cyber threats, enhancing their overall security posture.

7.3 Anomaly Detection Techniques

Anomaly detection is a crucial component of cyber threat hunting, as it enables organizations to identify deviations from established normal behaviors that may signify potential security incidents. This chapter delves into various anomaly detection techniques, exploring their methodologies, applications, and effectiveness in identifying threats within an organization's network and systems.

1. Overview of Anomaly Detection

Anomaly detection involves monitoring systems and user behaviors to identify patterns that significantly deviate from established norms. These deviations, or anomalies, can indicate various issues, including security breaches, system malfunctions, or operational inefficiencies. The objective of anomaly detection is to discern these irregular patterns, enabling security teams to investigate and mitigate potential threats promptly.

1.1 Types of Anomalies

Anomalies can be categorized into several types:

Point Anomalies: These are individual data points that significantly differ from the rest of the dataset. For example, a sudden spike in network traffic from a specific user may be classified as a point anomaly.

Contextual Anomalies: These anomalies depend on the context in which they occur. For instance, accessing sensitive data during non-business hours might be normal for some users but suspicious for others, depending on their typical behaviors.

Collective Anomalies: These consist of a group of data points that, when considered together, represent an abnormal pattern. For instance, a series of failed login attempts followed by a successful login could indicate a brute-force attack.

2. Anomaly Detection Techniques

There are several techniques for anomaly detection, each with its strengths and weaknesses. Here, we explore the most common methods employed in cybersecurity.

2.1 Statistical Techniques

Statistical methods are widely used for anomaly detection, leveraging mathematical models to identify deviations from expected behavior.

Z-Score Analysis: This technique calculates the z-score for data points, measuring how many standard deviations an element is from the mean. A high z-score indicates an anomaly. For example, if a user's login times fall outside the expected range, their behavior may trigger an alert.

Control Charts: Control charts monitor processes over time, plotting data points against predefined control limits. Any points outside these limits indicate a potential anomaly, such as unexpected surges in network traffic.

Regression Analysis: Regression models can predict expected behavior based on historical data. Any significant deviations from these predictions can be flagged as anomalies. For example, if a model predicts a certain number of user logins and actual logins exceed that number, further investigation is warranted.

2.2 Machine Learning Techniques

Machine learning techniques have gained prominence for their ability to adapt to dynamic environments and identify complex patterns.

Supervised Learning: In supervised learning, models are trained on labeled datasets that distinguish between normal and abnormal behaviors. Algorithms such as decision trees, support vector machines, and neural networks can classify data based on historical patterns. For example, a model might be trained to recognize typical file access patterns to identify unauthorized access attempts.

Unsupervised Learning: Unsupervised learning algorithms do not require labeled data, making them suitable for situations where normal behavior is not well-defined. Clustering techniques like K-means and hierarchical clustering can group similar data points together, with outliers being classified as anomalies. This method is useful for detecting unusual user behavior patterns that deviate from established norms.

Isolation Forest: This ensemble learning method identifies anomalies by randomly partitioning the dataset. Points that are isolated quickly from the rest of the data are considered anomalies. The isolation forest technique is effective in handling high-dimensional datasets and is often used in scenarios where the data distribution is unknown.

2.3 Rule-Based Techniques

Rule-based anomaly detection involves defining specific rules or thresholds that, when violated, indicate abnormal behavior.

Threshold-Based Detection: This approach establishes thresholds for specific metrics, such as the number of failed login attempts or the volume of data transfers. When these thresholds are exceeded, alerts are triggered for further investigation. For instance, if a user attempts to log in more than five times within a minute, this could indicate a brute-force attack.

Heuristic Rules: Heuristic rules are based on expert knowledge and predefined conditions that signal potential anomalies. For example, a heuristic rule may flag any access to sensitive data by a user who has not previously accessed such data.

2.4 Hybrid Techniques

Hybrid techniques combine multiple methods to enhance detection accuracy and reduce false positives.

Ensemble Methods: These approaches utilize multiple models or algorithms to improve detection performance. For example, combining supervised learning with statistical methods can yield more robust anomaly detection. By leveraging the strengths of each approach, security teams can improve their ability to identify and respond to threats.

Multi-Layered Detection: Implementing a multi-layered detection strategy, which combines behavioral analysis, machine learning, and rule-based techniques, can provide a more comprehensive view of potential anomalies. This approach enhances the chances of detecting sophisticated threats that may evade single-method detection systems.

3. Evaluating Anomaly Detection Techniques

When selecting and implementing anomaly detection techniques, organizations should consider several factors to evaluate their effectiveness:

3.1 Accuracy and Precision

The ability of an anomaly detection technique to accurately identify true anomalies while minimizing false positives is critical. Techniques with high precision reduce alert fatigue, allowing security teams to focus on genuine threats.

3.2 Adaptability

In dynamic environments, anomaly detection techniques must adapt to evolving user behaviors and system configurations. Machine learning techniques, particularly unsupervised learning, often provide better adaptability to changing conditions compared to static statistical methods.

3.3 Scalability

As organizations grow, the volume of data generated increases significantly. Anomaly detection techniques must be scalable to handle large datasets without compromising performance. Techniques such as isolation forests and ensemble methods can efficiently process high-dimensional data.

3.4 Real-Time Detection

For effective threat hunting, real-time anomaly detection is essential. Techniques that provide immediate alerts for abnormal behaviors enable security teams to respond quickly to potential threats, minimizing damage.

4. Challenges in Anomaly Detection

Despite the advancements in anomaly detection techniques, several challenges persist:

4.1 Data Quality and Availability

The effectiveness of anomaly detection largely depends on the quality and availability of data. Incomplete or inaccurate data can lead to misclassifications and missed threats. Organizations must prioritize data integrity and consistency for optimal results.

4.2 Evolving Threats

Adversaries continuously adapt their tactics to evade detection. As a result, anomaly detection techniques must evolve alongside emerging threats. Regular updates and retraining of machine learning models are crucial to maintaining effectiveness.

4.3 Insider Threats

Insider threats pose unique challenges for anomaly detection, as malicious insiders may exhibit behavior similar to legitimate users. This camouflage complicates the identification of true anomalies and necessitates a nuanced approach to detection.

Anomaly detection techniques play a vital role in the landscape of cyber threat hunting. By identifying deviations from established normal behaviors, organizations can proactively detect potential threats and respond swiftly. With a range of techniques available, from statistical and machine learning methods to rule-based and hybrid approaches, organizations can tailor their detection strategies to suit their unique environments. However, challenges such as data quality, evolving threats, and insider risks must be carefully managed to ensure the effectiveness of anomaly detection efforts. Ultimately, organizations that implement robust anomaly detection techniques will be better equipped to defend against the ever-evolving threat landscape, enhancing their overall cybersecurity posture.

8. Advanced Threat Hunting Techniques

As cyber threats continue to evolve, so must the strategies employed by threat hunters to stay one step ahead of malicious actors. In this chapter, we will delve into advanced threat hunting techniques that go beyond traditional methods, equipping security professionals with innovative tools and tactics to enhance their detection capabilities. We will explore threat emulation and simulation, discussing how these techniques allow teams to anticipate potential attack vectors and test their defenses against real-world scenarios. Additionally, we will examine the role of deception technology, including honeypots and decoy systems, in luring attackers and gathering intelligence on their methods. Furthermore, we will cover malware analysis, providing insights into reverse engineering and behavioral analysis of malicious code to better understand its impact and detection. By mastering these advanced techniques, threat hunters can strengthen their arsenal against evolving threats and significantly improve their organization's overall cybersecurity posture.

8.1 Threat Emulation and Simulation

Threat emulation and simulation are critical techniques in the field of cybersecurity, particularly for organizations seeking to enhance their threat hunting capabilities. By understanding and replicating the tactics, techniques, and procedures (TTPs) used by adversaries, security teams can improve their defenses, develop more effective response strategies, and better prepare for potential attacks. This chapter delves into the concepts of threat emulation and simulation, their methodologies, and their practical applications in strengthening cybersecurity postures.

1. Understanding Threat Emulation and Simulation

Threat emulation refers to the practice of mimicking the behaviors and tactics of real-world adversaries to identify vulnerabilities in an organization's defenses. It allows security teams to proactively test their security measures and improve their incident response plans by understanding how attackers might exploit weaknesses.

Threat simulation, on the other hand, encompasses a broader scope that includes not only emulating specific threats but also creating realistic attack scenarios to evaluate how an organization would respond. This can involve the use of simulations in tabletop exercises, penetration testing, and red team/blue team engagements.

1.1 Key Differences

While both concepts share the goal of enhancing cybersecurity resilience, they differ in focus:

Threat Emulation: Primarily focused on replicating specific adversarial behaviors and techniques to evaluate defenses against those specific threats.

Threat Simulation: Involves a wider range of activities, including comprehensive attack scenarios, to assess the effectiveness of security controls, detection capabilities, and response strategies.

2. The Importance of Threat Emulation and Simulation

As cyber threats continue to evolve in complexity and sophistication, organizations must adopt proactive measures to identify and mitigate potential risks. The importance of threat emulation and simulation can be summarized in the following points:

2.1 Identifying Vulnerabilities

By emulating real-world attack scenarios, organizations can uncover vulnerabilities within their systems, processes, and personnel. This proactive approach helps security teams to address weaknesses before they can be exploited by malicious actors.

2.2 Improving Incident Response

Threat simulation exercises provide security teams with practical experience in responding to attacks. By rehearsing their response plans in realistic scenarios, teams can identify gaps in their processes, improve communication, and enhance coordination among team members.

2.3 Testing Security Controls

Threat emulation enables organizations to evaluate the effectiveness of their security controls and detection mechanisms. By simulating attacks, security teams can assess whether their tools and processes are functioning as intended and identify areas for improvement.

2.4 Enhancing Security Awareness

Conducting threat emulation and simulation exercises raises awareness among employees about potential threats and the importance of cybersecurity. This can lead to a more security-conscious organizational culture and better preparedness against social engineering attacks.

3. Methodologies for Threat Emulation and Simulation

To effectively implement threat emulation and simulation, organizations can utilize a variety of methodologies and frameworks. These approaches typically involve planning, execution, and analysis phases.

3.1 Threat Intelligence Gathering

The foundation of effective threat emulation lies in understanding the TTPs of adversaries. Organizations should gather relevant threat intelligence, including:

- **Adversary Profiles**: Researching and identifying specific threat actors targeting the organization or industry.
- **Tactics, Techniques, and Procedures (TTPs):** Analyzing documented TTPs associated with known adversaries to inform emulation efforts.
- **Recent Attack Trends**: Staying updated on the latest cyber threats and vulnerabilities to adapt emulation scenarios accordingly.

3.2 Planning and Scoping

Before conducting emulation or simulation exercises, organizations must plan and scope the effort. This includes:

- **Defining Objectives**: Clearly outlining the goals of the exercise, such as identifying vulnerabilities, testing incident response, or evaluating security controls.
- **Selecting Scenarios**: Choosing specific attack scenarios based on identified threats, organizational risks, and past incidents.
- **Identifying Participants**: Determining which team members will participate in the exercise, including representatives from security, IT, and other relevant departments.

3.3 Execution of Emulation and Simulation

The execution phase involves carrying out the planned emulation or simulation scenarios. Key activities include:

Conducting Penetration Testing: Security professionals (often referred to as ethical hackers) simulate attacks on systems to identify vulnerabilities and exploit them to evaluate the effectiveness of security measures.

Red Team/Blue Team Exercises: In this approach, a red team (attackers) conducts simulated attacks against a blue team (defenders). This dynamic interaction helps both teams understand their strengths and weaknesses in real-time.

Tabletop Exercises: These facilitated discussions involve key stakeholders walking through hypothetical attack scenarios to assess the organization's response procedures and decision-making processes.

3.4 Analysis and Reporting

After the emulation or simulation exercise, organizations must analyze the results and compile reports to inform future actions. This phase involves:

Identifying Findings: Documenting vulnerabilities, weaknesses, and gaps in incident response discovered during the exercise.

Providing Recommendations: Offering actionable recommendations for improving security controls, incident response plans, and training programs based on the findings.

Conducting Debriefs: Holding debriefing sessions with participants to discuss lessons learned and areas for improvement, fostering a culture of continuous learning.

4. Tools and Technologies for Threat Emulation and Simulation

Various tools and technologies can assist organizations in conducting threat emulation and simulation exercises effectively. These may include:

4.1 Threat Emulation Platforms

Attack Simulation Tools: Solutions such as MITRE ATT&CK Navigator and Caldera allow organizations to model and execute various attack scenarios based on documented TTPs, helping to evaluate detection and response capabilities.

Penetration Testing Frameworks: Tools like Metasploit, Cobalt Strike, and Burp Suite enable security professionals to perform simulated attacks and assess vulnerabilities within systems and applications.

4.2 Security Orchestration and Automation

SOAR Solutions: Security Orchestration, Automation, and Response (SOAR) platforms can automate various aspects of threat simulation, including data collection, analysis, and incident response workflows, improving efficiency and effectiveness.

4.3 Learning Management Systems

Security Awareness Training Platforms: Tools that provide cybersecurity training and simulations for employees can enhance security awareness and preparedness against social engineering attacks.

5. Challenges in Threat Emulation and Simulation

While threat emulation and simulation offer significant benefits, organizations may encounter several challenges:

5.1 Resource Constraints

Conducting comprehensive emulation and simulation exercises requires significant resources, including skilled personnel, tools, and time. Organizations must allocate sufficient resources to ensure effective execution.

5.2 Organizational Buy-In

Securing buy-in from leadership and various stakeholders is crucial for the success of emulation and simulation exercises. Resistance or lack of support can hinder the planning and execution of these activities.

5.3 Scope Creep

As exercises progress, there may be a tendency to expand the scope beyond the original objectives, potentially leading to confusion and ineffective outcomes. Clearly defined objectives and strict adherence to the scope are essential for successful exercises.

Threat emulation and simulation are invaluable techniques for enhancing an organization's cybersecurity posture. By replicating the behaviors and tactics of real-world adversaries, security teams can identify vulnerabilities, test incident response plans, and improve security awareness. Through careful planning, execution, and analysis, organizations can effectively leverage threat emulation and simulation to prepare for potential attacks, bolster their defenses, and foster a culture of continuous improvement. As the threat landscape continues to evolve, investing in these proactive approaches will be critical for organizations seeking to stay one step ahead of adversaries and protect their digital assets.

8.2 Deception Technology and Honeypots

In an era of increasing cyber threats, organizations are seeking innovative strategies to protect their networks and data. One such strategy is the use of deception technology, which includes honeypots and honeynets. These tools create deceptive environments to lure attackers, gather intelligence, and enhance cybersecurity defenses. This chapter explores the concepts of deception technology and honeypots, their methodologies, applications, and benefits, as well as the challenges associated with their implementation.

1. Understanding Deception Technology

Deception technology is a proactive cybersecurity strategy designed to mislead attackers by creating traps or decoys that mimic legitimate systems or data. The primary goal is to divert attackers' attention away from real assets, allowing organizations to detect, analyze, and respond to threats more effectively.

1.1 Key Concepts of Deception Technology

Decoys and Traps: Deception technology involves the deployment of decoy systems (e.g., honeypots) that appear legitimate to attackers. These decoys can be designed to look like valuable assets, enticing adversaries to interact with them.

Threat Intelligence Gathering: By monitoring attacker interactions with decoys, organizations can collect valuable intelligence on tactics, techniques, and procedures (TTPs) employed by adversaries. This information can inform future defenses and incident response strategies.

Proactive Defense: Rather than waiting for attacks to occur on real assets, deception technology enables organizations to take a proactive stance, identifying and mitigating threats before they can cause damage.

2. Honeypots: The Backbone of Deception Technology

Honeypots are decoy systems intentionally designed to be vulnerable and enticing to attackers. They serve various purposes, including threat detection, research, and analysis. This section outlines the types, architecture, and operational aspects of honeypots.

2.1 Types of Honeypots

Production Honeypots: Deployed within an organization's production environment, these honeypots aim to detect and analyze real attacks targeting legitimate assets. They are often low-interaction honeypots, providing limited functionality to prevent exploitation.

Research Honeypots: These honeypots are designed for research purposes, allowing organizations to study attacker behavior and gather intelligence on emerging threats. Research honeypots typically offer more interaction and mimic critical systems.

High-Interaction Honeypots: These honeypots provide a fully operational system with realistic vulnerabilities, allowing attackers to interact with the environment extensively. While they offer rich data, they also pose higher risks if not managed properly.

2.2 Honeypot Architecture

The architecture of a honeypot can vary based on its purpose and design. Key components typically include:

Decoy Services: Honeypots emulate services and applications commonly found in the production environment, enticing attackers to engage with them.

Monitoring and Logging: Comprehensive monitoring tools are essential to capture attacker actions, log interactions, and record the techniques employed during attacks.

Isolation: Honeypots should be isolated from the production network to prevent attackers from pivoting to legitimate systems. Isolation can be achieved through network segmentation and strict access controls.

2.3 Operational Considerations

When deploying honeypots, organizations should consider the following operational aspects:

Deployment Strategy: Organizations must determine where to deploy honeypots based on their network architecture, assets, and potential attack vectors.

Maintenance and Updates: Regular maintenance and updates are essential to keep honeypots relevant and effective. This includes patching vulnerabilities and ensuring that honeypots remain appealing to attackers.

Data Analysis and Response: Organizations should establish processes for analyzing data collected from honeypots and integrating findings into threat intelligence and incident response strategies.

3. Benefits of Deception Technology and Honeypots

Deception technology and honeypots offer several significant benefits for organizations seeking to enhance their cybersecurity posture:

3.1 Enhanced Threat Detection

By luring attackers into honeypots, organizations can detect malicious activities earlier in the attack lifecycle. This early detection enables quicker response times and reduces the likelihood of successful breaches.

3.2 Improved Threat Intelligence

The data collected from honeypots provides invaluable insights into attacker tactics and techniques. Organizations can analyze this information to enhance their threat models and improve their overall security posture.

3.3 Reduced Attack Surface

By diverting attackers away from real assets, honeypots help to reduce the attack surface, minimizing the chances of successful breaches and data theft.

3.4 Cost-Effective Security Measure

Deception technology can be a cost-effective addition to an organization's security arsenal. While initial setup may require investment, the long-term benefits in threat detection and incident response can lead to reduced costs associated with breaches and incidents.

4. Challenges of Implementing Deception Technology and Honeypots

While deception technology and honeypots offer numerous advantages, organizations may face several challenges during implementation:

4.1 Complexity of Deployment

Setting up honeypots requires careful planning and technical expertise. Organizations must consider their network architecture and determine the best placement for honeypots to maximize effectiveness.

4.2 Risk of Misuse

If not properly isolated, honeypots may inadvertently allow attackers to access legitimate systems. Organizations must implement strict access controls and monitoring to mitigate this risk.

4.3 Managing False Positives

Organizations may encounter false positives when monitoring honeypots, leading to unnecessary alerts. Establishing clear baselines for normal behavior and refining detection mechanisms can help minimize this issue.

4.4 Resource Intensive

Managing honeypots requires ongoing attention, including regular updates and monitoring. Organizations must allocate sufficient resources to maintain their honeypots effectively.

5. Future Trends in Deception Technology

As the cybersecurity landscape continues to evolve, several trends may influence the future of deception technology and honeypots:

5.1 Integration with AI and Machine Learning

Artificial intelligence and machine learning can enhance the effectiveness of deception technology by automating data analysis and identifying patterns in attacker behavior. This integration can lead to more adaptive and responsive honeypots.

5.2 Greater Customization

Organizations may increasingly seek customized honeypots tailored to their specific environments and threat landscapes. Customization can improve the relevance and effectiveness of deception strategies.

5.3 Collaboration and Information Sharing

Collaboration among organizations to share threat intelligence gathered from honeypots can enhance the overall effectiveness of deception technology. Industry-wide sharing of tactics and techniques can improve collective defenses.

Deception technology and honeypots play a vital role in enhancing an organization's cybersecurity posture. By creating realistic decoy environments, organizations can lure attackers, gather intelligence, and improve their incident response capabilities. While challenges exist in deployment and management, the benefits of early threat detection, enhanced threat intelligence, and reduced attack surface make deception technology a compelling addition to modern cybersecurity strategies. As cyber threats continue to evolve, investing in deception technology will be essential for organizations aiming to stay ahead of adversaries and protect their critical assets.

8.3 Malware Analysis for Threat Hunters

Malware analysis is a crucial component of threat hunting that empowers security professionals to understand and mitigate the threats posed by malicious software. With cybercriminals continuously evolving their tactics, understanding malware behaviors, techniques, and signatures is essential for threat hunters to effectively defend against potential breaches. This chapter delves into the methodologies and techniques of malware analysis, its significance in threat hunting, and how threat hunters can leverage this knowledge to enhance their cybersecurity posture.

1. Understanding Malware Analysis

Malware analysis involves the systematic examination of malicious software to determine its capabilities, behaviors, and impact on systems and networks. This process is critical for identifying malware signatures, understanding how malware operates, and developing effective detection and remediation strategies.

1.1 Types of Malware Analysis

Malware analysis can be broadly categorized into two primary types:

Static Analysis: This involves examining the malware without executing it. Security analysts review the code, binaries, and file structure of the malware to identify characteristics, patterns, and potential indicators of compromise (IOCs). Static analysis is often conducted using disassemblers, decompilers, and other analysis tools.

Dynamic Analysis: This approach involves executing the malware in a controlled environment (sandbox) to observe its behavior in real-time. Analysts monitor the interactions between the malware and the operating system, network, and other applications to understand how it operates, what resources it uses, and how it communicates with command-and-control (C2) servers.

1.2 The Importance of Malware Analysis in Threat Hunting

Understanding malware is essential for threat hunters for several reasons:

Identifying Indicators of Compromise (IOCs): Analyzing malware can help security teams develop IOCs, which are crucial for detecting malicious activity and improving incident response.

Threat Intelligence Development: Knowledge gained from malware analysis can contribute to threat intelligence efforts, helping organizations understand emerging threats and trends in the cyber landscape.

Enhancing Detection Capabilities: Insights from malware analysis can be integrated into security tools and frameworks, improving the detection of similar threats in the future.

2. The Malware Analysis Process

Conducting malware analysis involves several key steps. Each step is crucial for gaining comprehensive insights into the malware's capabilities and behaviors.

2.1 Preparation and Environment Setup

Before analyzing malware, security analysts must set up a controlled environment to mitigate risks. This typically involves:

Creating a Sandbox: A virtual machine or isolated environment is set up to safely execute and monitor the malware. Sandboxes should have restricted internet access to prevent malware from spreading.

Equipping the Analysis Environment: Analysts should equip their sandbox with necessary tools, including debuggers, disassemblers, network monitoring tools, and forensic analysis software.

2.2 Static Analysis Techniques

During static analysis, analysts review the malware without executing it. Common techniques include:

File Inspection: Analysts examine file headers, metadata, and signatures to identify the type of malware, its origin, and its potential purpose.

Code Analysis: Disassemblers such as IDA Pro or Ghidra allow analysts to view the malware's assembly code, enabling them to understand its structure and logic.

Behavioral Indicators: Analysts identify patterns and strings within the code that may indicate malicious behavior, such as C2 URLs or commands.

2.3 Dynamic Analysis Techniques

Dynamic analysis involves executing the malware in a controlled environment to observe its behavior. Key techniques include:

Process Monitoring: Analysts monitor processes created by the malware, tracking CPU and memory usage to identify abnormal behaviors.

Network Traffic Analysis: Tools like Wireshark are used to capture and analyze network traffic generated by the malware, revealing communication with C2 servers and other malicious activity.

File System Changes: Analysts observe any changes made by the malware to the file system, such as the creation, modification, or deletion of files and registry entries.

2.4 Reporting and Documentation

After completing the analysis, analysts document their findings in a comprehensive report. Key components of the report include:

Malware Overview: A description of the malware, its variants, and known behaviors.

IOCs: Indicators of compromise identified during the analysis, including file hashes, IP addresses, and domain names.

Recommendations: Suggested mitigation strategies, detection methods, and remediation steps for affected systems.

3. Tools for Malware Analysis

A variety of tools are available for malware analysis, each serving specific purposes within the analysis process. Key categories of tools include:

3.1 Static Analysis Tools

Disassemblers and Decompilers: Tools like IDA Pro, Ghidra, and Binary Ninja allow analysts to convert machine code into a human-readable format for analysis.

Hex Editors: Software like HxD enables analysts to inspect the raw binary data of malware files.

VirusTotal: An online service that analyzes files and URLs for malware detection using various antivirus engines and tools.

3.2 Dynamic Analysis Tools

Sandbox Environments: Tools like Cuckoo Sandbox and Joe Sandbox allow analysts to safely execute malware and observe its behavior in a controlled setting.

Network Monitoring Tools: Wireshark and Fiddler help capture and analyze network traffic generated by the malware.

Process Monitoring Tools: Sysinternals Suite (e.g., Process Monitor) provides insights into processes and file system activity in real-time.

4. Challenges in Malware Analysis

While malware analysis is crucial for effective threat hunting, it is not without challenges:

4.1 Evasion Techniques

Many modern malware variants employ evasion techniques to avoid detection during analysis. These may include code obfuscation, anti-debugging measures, and polymorphic behaviors, making analysis more challenging.

4.2 Resource Intensity

Malware analysis can be resource-intensive, requiring significant time and expertise. Analysts may face pressure to deliver timely insights while managing complex and sophisticated malware variants.

4.3 Constant Evolution of Malware

The malware landscape is continuously evolving, with new variants emerging frequently. Threat hunters must stay updated on the latest trends and techniques used by cybercriminals to maintain effective defenses.

5. Leveraging Malware Analysis for Threat Hunting

Threat hunters can leverage insights gained from malware analysis to enhance their overall threat detection and response capabilities. Key strategies include:

5.1 Integrating IOCs into Detection Systems

Once IOCs are identified during malware analysis, they should be integrated into security monitoring systems, such as SIEM (Security Information and Event Management) solutions, to improve detection capabilities.

5.2 Developing Threat Intelligence Feeds

Threat hunters can contribute to threat intelligence feeds by sharing findings from malware analysis, helping organizations understand emerging threats and improving collective defenses.

5.3 Continuous Learning and Adaptation

As the threat landscape evolves, threat hunters should adopt a continuous learning approach, staying informed about the latest malware trends, techniques, and behaviors. Engaging in communities, attending conferences, and participating in training can help enhance skills and knowledge.

Malware analysis is a fundamental skill for threat hunters, providing critical insights into the behaviors and tactics of cyber adversaries. By understanding how malware operates and leveraging this knowledge, threat hunters can enhance their detection capabilities, develop effective incident response strategies, and stay one step ahead of evolving threats. As the landscape of malware continues to evolve, a commitment to ongoing education and adaptation will be essential for security professionals seeking to protect their organizations from malicious attacks. Through effective malware analysis, threat hunters can significantly improve their organization's cybersecurity posture and resilience against cyber threats.

9. Incident Response and Threat Hunting Integration

The integration of incident response and threat hunting is crucial for organizations aiming to establish a comprehensive cybersecurity strategy that effectively identifies and mitigates threats. In this chapter, we will explore the symbiotic relationship between these two disciplines, highlighting how proactive threat hunting can enhance incident response efforts. We will discuss the importance of collaboration between threat hunters and incident responders, emphasizing the need for clear communication and shared objectives in the face of cyber incidents. Additionally, we will examine how findings from threat hunting initiatives can inform and shape incident response plans, allowing organizations to anticipate potential threats and develop more effective mitigation strategies. We will also cover the critical role of documentation and reporting, illustrating how to capture and analyze hunting results to improve response capabilities. By understanding and implementing the integration of threat hunting and incident response, organizations can create a more agile and resilient cybersecurity framework, capable of swiftly addressing the challenges posed by today's dynamic threat landscape.

9.1 Collaboration Between Threat Hunters and Incident Response

In the dynamic landscape of cybersecurity, the collaboration between threat hunters and incident response (IR) teams is crucial for effectively detecting, analyzing, and mitigating cyber threats. As organizations face increasingly sophisticated attacks, the need for seamless cooperation between these two functions has become more pronounced. This chapter explores the importance of collaboration, outlines the roles and responsibilities of both teams, and discusses best practices for enhancing their synergy.

1. Understanding the Roles

1.1 Threat Hunters

Threat hunters proactively search for indicators of compromise (IOCs) and malicious activities within an organization's network and systems. Their primary goal is to identify threats before they escalate into incidents, utilizing a combination of threat intelligence, behavioral analysis, and advanced tools.

Key Responsibilities:

Identifying Emerging Threats: Threat hunters leverage threat intelligence and monitoring tools to stay informed about new attack vectors and techniques used by adversaries.

Hypothesis Testing: They formulate hypotheses based on potential threat scenarios and investigate their validity by analyzing logs, network traffic, and endpoint activities.

Data Enrichment: Threat hunters gather and enrich data from various sources, including SIEM systems, threat intelligence feeds, and external databases, to enhance their analysis.

1.2 Incident Response Teams

Incident response teams are responsible for managing and mitigating security incidents after they occur. Their focus is on minimizing the impact of an incident, restoring normal operations, and implementing lessons learned to prevent future occurrences.

Key Responsibilities:

Incident Detection and Containment: IR teams monitor alerts and incidents to quickly identify and contain security breaches, preventing further damage.

Root Cause Analysis: They conduct investigations to determine the source and impact of an incident, identifying vulnerabilities that were exploited.

Post-Incident Review: After an incident is resolved, IR teams conduct a post-incident review to document findings and improve response strategies.

2. Importance of Collaboration

The collaboration between threat hunters and incident response teams is essential for several reasons:

2.1 Enhancing Detection Capabilities

When threat hunters and incident response teams work together, they can develop more effective detection capabilities. Threat hunters can provide insights into potential attack patterns and IOCs, which can inform the incident response team's monitoring and alerting strategies. This proactive approach allows organizations to detect threats before they result in significant incidents.

2.2 Streamlining Incident Response

A collaborative environment fosters better communication and information sharing between teams, enabling quicker responses to security incidents. By understanding the threat landscape and the types of attacks they are likely to face, incident response teams can prioritize their efforts and allocate resources more effectively.

2.3 Building a Holistic Security Posture

Collaboration promotes a more holistic approach to cybersecurity. By combining the proactive efforts of threat hunters with the reactive measures of incident response, organizations can create a more resilient security posture. This synergy helps in understanding the entire attack lifecycle, from detection to response and recovery.

3. Best Practices for Collaboration

To maximize the effectiveness of collaboration between threat hunters and incident response teams, organizations should adopt several best practices:

3.1 Establish Clear Communication Channels

Creating formal communication channels is vital for ensuring that both teams can easily share information and insights. Regular meetings, joint briefings, and collaborative tools can facilitate information exchange and foster a shared understanding of the threat landscape.

3.2 Develop Integrated Workflows

Organizations should define and document workflows that outline how threat hunters and incident response teams will collaborate during incidents. This includes establishing clear procedures for escalating threats, sharing IOCs, and conducting joint investigations. An integrated workflow ensures that both teams are aligned in their efforts and can respond effectively to threats.

3.3 Conduct Joint Training and Exercises

Regular training sessions and tabletop exercises that involve both teams can enhance their collaboration skills and improve their ability to work together under pressure. These exercises provide opportunities to practice communication, decision-making, and coordination during simulated incidents, reinforcing teamwork and shared objectives.

3.4 Share Insights and Findings

Both teams should regularly share insights, findings, and lessons learned from their respective activities. Threat hunters can share intelligence gathered during hunts, while incident response teams can provide feedback on incidents and their resolutions. This exchange of information enhances the overall knowledge base of both teams and contributes to continuous improvement.

3.5 Utilize Shared Tools and Technologies

Investing in shared tools and technologies that facilitate collaboration can enhance efficiency. For instance, using a centralized SIEM platform allows both teams to access the same data, enabling them to analyze threats and incidents from a unified perspective. Collaborative platforms for threat intelligence sharing and incident management can further streamline workflows.

4. Real-World Examples of Collaboration

Many organizations have successfully implemented collaborative approaches between threat hunters and incident response teams, yielding significant benefits:

4.1 Case Study: Financial Institution

A financial institution faced a sophisticated phishing attack that bypassed traditional defenses. The threat hunting team detected unusual user behavior and shared their findings with the incident response team. Together, they conducted a joint investigation, identified the compromised accounts, and quickly implemented measures to contain the threat. This collaboration not only minimized the damage but also informed future training programs for employees on recognizing phishing attempts.

4.2 Case Study: Healthcare Organization

A healthcare organization experienced a ransomware attack that encrypted critical patient data. The incident response team acted quickly to contain the threat, while the threat hunting team analyzed the malware strain involved in the attack. By sharing their insights, they identified specific vulnerabilities in their infrastructure and implemented targeted defenses to prevent similar incidents in the future. This collaborative approach led to a significant reduction in the organization's risk exposure.

Collaboration between threat hunters and incident response teams is essential for effective cybersecurity. By working together, these teams can enhance detection capabilities, streamline incident response, and build a more resilient security posture. Implementing best practices for collaboration, such as establishing clear communication channels, developing integrated workflows, and conducting joint training, can significantly improve an organization's ability to detect and respond to threats. As the cyber threat landscape continues to evolve, fostering collaboration between these two critical functions will be vital for maintaining strong defenses against sophisticated attacks. Organizations that prioritize collaboration will be better positioned to navigate the complex challenges of cybersecurity and protect their assets from harm.

9.2 Using Hunt Findings for Response Planning

In the evolving landscape of cybersecurity, the ability to respond effectively to threats is paramount for organizations. Proactive threat hunting not only enhances detection capabilities but also plays a critical role in informing and shaping incident response strategies. This chapter explores how findings from threat hunting activities can be leveraged for effective response planning, enabling organizations to be better prepared for potential incidents.

1. The Role of Threat Hunting in Incident Response

Threat hunting is an active and iterative process where security professionals search for signs of malicious activity within a network before an incident occurs. The insights gained from these hunts provide valuable intelligence that can significantly influence how organizations prepare for and respond to security incidents.

1.1 Identifying Vulnerabilities

During threat hunting activities, hunters often uncover vulnerabilities and weaknesses in the organization's security posture. These findings highlight areas that require immediate attention, allowing incident response teams to prioritize their efforts based on actual risk rather than hypothetical scenarios.

1.2 Understanding Adversarial Techniques

Threat hunters analyze various tactics, techniques, and procedures (TTPs) used by adversaries. By documenting these findings, organizations can develop a more comprehensive understanding of how attackers operate, allowing incident response teams to anticipate and mitigate potential attacks effectively.

1.3 Creating Actionable Intelligence

The data and insights collected during threat hunting can be transformed into actionable intelligence. This intelligence can guide incident response planning, helping teams develop specific strategies to address identified threats.

2. Leveraging Hunt Findings for Response Planning

To maximize the value of threat hunting findings in response planning, organizations should adopt several key strategies:

2.1 Prioritizing Response Strategies

Based on the findings from threat hunting, organizations can prioritize their response strategies. Here are some approaches to consider:

Risk Assessment: Evaluate the severity of identified threats and vulnerabilities. High-risk findings should be addressed promptly, while lower-risk items can be scheduled for longer-term remediation.

Resource Allocation: Allocate resources more effectively based on the threat landscape revealed by hunt findings. This might involve assigning specific personnel to focus on critical vulnerabilities or investing in additional tools to enhance defenses.

Defining Response Protocols: Use the insights gained from threat hunting to define specific response protocols for various scenarios. For example, if certain malware strains are frequently detected, the incident response team can develop standardized procedures for addressing those specific threats.

2.2 Integrating Threat Intelligence

Findings from threat hunting activities should be integrated into the organization's threat intelligence framework. This integration can take several forms:

Threat Intelligence Feeds: Incorporate hunt findings into existing threat intelligence feeds to enhance the overall intelligence landscape. By sharing insights on IOCs, TTPs, and emerging threats, organizations can create a more robust defensive posture.

Automated Detection: Use findings from threat hunting to inform automated detection mechanisms. Security tools can be fine-tuned to look for specific patterns identified during hunts, enabling quicker responses to potential threats.

Collaboration with External Intelligence Sources: Engage with external threat intelligence sources to enrich internal findings. This collaborative approach allows organizations to contextualize their threat landscape within broader industry trends.

2.3 Developing Incident Response Playbooks

Incident response playbooks are essential for guiding teams through the response process during security incidents. Threat hunting findings can significantly enhance these playbooks in the following ways:

Scenario-Based Playbooks: Use insights from threat hunting to create scenario-based playbooks that outline response steps for specific threats. For instance, if hunting activities reveal a spike in ransomware activity, the playbook can include detailed steps for isolating affected systems, communication protocols, and recovery procedures.

Continuous Updates: Ensure that incident response playbooks are regularly updated with new information from threat hunting activities. This ongoing refinement keeps the playbooks relevant and effective, reflecting the latest threats and tactics used by adversaries.

Testing and Validation: Conduct tabletop exercises using the findings from threat hunting to test the effectiveness of incident response playbooks. This practice helps teams identify gaps in their response plans and refine their strategies accordingly.

3. Continuous Improvement Cycle

The relationship between threat hunting and incident response is iterative, fostering a continuous improvement cycle:

3.1 Feedback Loop

Establish a feedback loop where incident response teams provide insights back to the threat hunting team. After an incident is resolved, hunters can analyze the response efforts, identify areas for improvement, and adapt their hunting strategies accordingly.

3.2 Performance Metrics

Develop performance metrics to evaluate the effectiveness of the response strategies influenced by threat hunting findings. This includes measuring response times, recovery times, and the success rate of mitigating threats based on identified vulnerabilities.

3.3 Adaptive Strategies

Cyber threats are constantly evolving, necessitating adaptive strategies. Organizations should ensure that both threat hunting and incident response processes remain flexible and responsive to new information, allowing for adjustments based on emerging threats.

4. Case Study: Real-World Application

A notable example of effectively using threat hunting findings for response planning can be observed in a multinational retail corporation that faced repeated malware attacks. The threat hunting team identified several indicators of compromise linked to a specific malware variant that was being exploited by cybercriminals.

Actions Taken:

Incident Response Playbook Development: Based on the identified malware's TTPs, the incident response team developed a comprehensive playbook detailing response steps for similar attacks.

Threat Intelligence Integration: The organization integrated the hunt findings into their threat intelligence feeds, allowing for improved detection and quicker responses.

Employee Training: Recognizing that many attacks originated from social engineering tactics, the organization conducted training sessions to educate employees on identifying phishing attempts and reporting suspicious activities.

Outcome:

When a subsequent attack attempt occurred, the organization was able to detect and contain the threat quickly, significantly minimizing potential damage. The insights gained from the prior threat hunting activities informed the response strategies, demonstrating the effectiveness of integrating hunting findings into incident response planning.

Leveraging findings from threat hunting activities is essential for effective response planning in cybersecurity. By prioritizing response strategies, integrating threat intelligence, and developing adaptive incident response playbooks, organizations can significantly enhance their preparedness for potential security incidents. The iterative relationship between threat hunting and incident response fosters continuous improvement, ensuring that organizations remain resilient against the ever-evolving threat landscape. As threats become more sophisticated, the collaboration between these two critical functions will be pivotal in maintaining a strong security posture and effectively mitigating risks.

9.3 Documentation and Reporting of Hunt Results

Effective documentation and reporting of hunt results are critical components of a successful threat hunting program. These processes not only provide a historical record of findings but also facilitate communication with stakeholders and inform strategic decision-making. In this chapter, we will explore the best practices for documenting and reporting hunt results, the significance of these activities, and the tools and techniques that can enhance the effectiveness of the documentation process.

1. The Importance of Documentation and Reporting

Documentation and reporting serve multiple purposes in threat hunting:

1.1 Creating a Knowledge Repository

Proper documentation creates a knowledge repository that can be referenced in future hunting activities and incident responses. It ensures that valuable insights, patterns, and findings are not lost and can be utilized to inform future strategies.

1.2 Enhancing Collaboration and Communication

Well-documented hunt results facilitate better communication and collaboration among teams. By providing clear and concise reports, threat hunters can effectively share findings with incident response teams, management, and other stakeholders, ensuring everyone is on the same page regarding the organization's threat landscape.

1.3 Informing Risk Management and Compliance

Detailed reporting helps organizations assess their risk posture and compliance status. Documentation of threats, vulnerabilities, and hunting efforts can be invaluable for risk assessments and regulatory compliance, providing evidence of proactive security measures.

2. Best Practices for Documentation

To maximize the effectiveness of documentation in threat hunting, organizations should adhere to several best practices:

2.1 Standardized Templates

Develop standardized templates for documenting hunt findings. These templates should include sections for the following:

Executive Summary: A high-level overview of the hunt findings, suitable for management and non-technical stakeholders.

Objectives and Scope: Clearly outline the goals of the hunt, the specific areas investigated, and any limitations encountered.

Findings: Document detailed findings, including IOCs, TTPs, and any identified vulnerabilities. Each finding should be accompanied by context explaining its significance.

Recommendations: Provide actionable recommendations based on the findings to address identified risks and enhance the organization's security posture.

Appendices: Include any supporting documentation, such as raw data, logs, or visualizations, that may be relevant to the findings.

2.2 Timeliness

Ensure that documentation is completed in a timely manner. Hunt findings should be documented as soon as possible after the analysis to maintain accuracy and relevance. Delayed documentation can lead to forgotten details and reduced effectiveness in communicating findings.

2.3 Version Control

Implement a version control system for documentation. This allows teams to track changes made to hunt reports over time and ensures that everyone is working from the most current information. Version control is especially important when dealing with ongoing investigations where findings may evolve.

2.4 Clear Language and Visuals

Use clear and concise language in documentation. Avoid jargon and technical terms that may be unfamiliar to non-technical stakeholders. Incorporating visuals, such as charts, graphs, and infographics, can also enhance comprehension and engagement with the findings.

3. Reporting Hunt Results

Effective reporting of hunt results is just as important as documentation. Here are key considerations for reporting:

3.1 Audience Awareness

Tailor reports to the specific audience. Consider the technical proficiency of the readers and adjust the depth of information accordingly. For instance:

Management Reports: Focus on high-level insights, risks, and recommendations for improving security posture, avoiding technical jargon.

Technical Reports: Provide in-depth analysis, technical details, and specific IOCs relevant to security operations and incident response teams.

3.2 Regular Updates

Establish a regular cadence for reporting hunt results. Frequent updates help keep stakeholders informed about emerging threats, ongoing investigations, and progress made in addressing identified vulnerabilities. Consider creating a quarterly or monthly report that summarizes key findings and trends.

3.3 Utilizing Dashboards

Consider using dashboards to present hunt results in real-time. Dashboards can provide visualizations of key metrics, such as the number of threats identified, trends over time, and the status of ongoing investigations. This approach enhances accessibility and allows stakeholders to engage with the data interactively.

3.4 Incorporating Feedback

Seek feedback on reports from stakeholders to improve future reporting efforts. Understanding the preferences and requirements of the audience can help tailor reports to better meet their needs.

4. Tools and Techniques for Documentation and Reporting

Utilizing the right tools can streamline the documentation and reporting processes:

4.1 Documentation Management Systems

Implement a documentation management system that allows for easy storage, retrieval, and version control of hunt findings. Tools like Confluence, SharePoint, or Google Drive can facilitate collaboration among team members and ensure that documentation is readily accessible.

4.2 Incident Management Platforms

Use incident management platforms that support documentation and reporting functionalities. Tools like Jira, ServiceNow, or PagerDuty can integrate documentation into incident workflows, making it easier to correlate findings with incidents.

4.3 Data Visualization Tools

Incorporate data visualization tools, such as Tableau, Power BI, or Grafana, to create compelling visual representations of hunt findings. These tools can help convey complex data in an easily digestible format, making it more engaging for stakeholders.

4.4 Automation Tools

Consider automating parts of the documentation and reporting process. Scripts or automation tools can help generate reports based on predefined templates, reducing the time and effort required for documentation.

5. Case Study: Effective Documentation and Reporting

A leading telecommunications company faced challenges in effectively documenting and reporting its threat hunting activities. With multiple teams involved and varying levels of technical expertise, findings were often lost in translation or not communicated effectively.

Actions Taken:

Standardized Reporting Template: The company developed a standardized reporting template that included sections for executive summaries, detailed findings, and recommendations.

Regular Reporting Schedule: A monthly reporting schedule was established to ensure consistent communication of hunt results to all stakeholders.

Visualization Dashboards: The organization implemented a dashboard to visualize trends in threats and vulnerabilities, allowing stakeholders to easily access real-time data.

Outcome:

As a result of these initiatives, the telecommunications company significantly improved its ability to communicate hunt findings. Stakeholders reported greater awareness of the threat landscape, and the incident response team was better equipped to address vulnerabilities. This holistic approach to documentation and reporting fostered a proactive security culture within the organization.

Documentation and reporting of hunt results are vital components of an effective threat hunting program. By creating a structured approach to documenting findings, utilizing clear and concise reporting, and leveraging appropriate tools, organizations can enhance communication, inform strategic decisions, and ultimately improve their cybersecurity posture. In an environment where threats are constantly evolving, the ability to capture and communicate insights from threat hunting activities will be critical for organizations seeking to stay ahead of adversaries and protect their assets.

10. Measuring and Improving Threat Hunting Effectiveness

To ensure the success and continuous improvement of a threat hunting program, organizations must establish metrics that accurately measure its effectiveness and impact. In this chapter, we will delve into key performance indicators (KPIs) that help assess the success of threat hunting initiatives, including detection rates, time to detection, and the number of incidents averted. We will also discuss qualitative measures, such as the quality of intelligence gathered and the effectiveness of responses to identified threats. Additionally, we will explore strategies for fostering a culture of continuous improvement, emphasizing the importance of regular assessments, feedback loops, and training opportunities for threat hunters. By implementing a systematic approach to measuring and enhancing threat hunting effectiveness, organizations can adapt to emerging threats, refine their tactics, and ultimately strengthen their overall cybersecurity posture.

10.1 Key Performance Indicators for Threat Hunting

As organizations increasingly recognize the importance of proactive threat hunting, establishing effective Key Performance Indicators (KPIs) becomes crucial. KPIs provide a measurable way to assess the effectiveness of threat hunting efforts, allowing teams to refine their strategies, allocate resources efficiently, and demonstrate the value of their activities to stakeholders. This chapter explores the essential KPIs for threat hunting, how to implement them, and how to interpret the results to enhance threat hunting programs.

1. Understanding Key Performance Indicators (KPIs)

Key Performance Indicators (KPIs) are quantifiable metrics that help organizations evaluate their success in achieving specific objectives. In the context of threat hunting, KPIs serve several purposes:

Measuring Effectiveness: KPIs help gauge the success of threat hunting initiatives by providing data-driven insights into the outcomes of hunting activities.

Informing Decision-Making: By analyzing KPI data, security teams can make informed decisions regarding resource allocation, strategy adjustments, and process improvements.

Demonstrating Value: KPIs provide concrete evidence of the effectiveness of threat hunting efforts, helping security teams communicate their value to upper management and stakeholders.

2. Essential KPIs for Threat Hunting

To effectively measure threat hunting performance, organizations should consider the following key performance indicators:

2.1 Detections Per Hunt

Description: This KPI measures the number of threats or anomalies detected during a specific hunting activity. It helps quantify the effectiveness of the hunt.

Calculation: Total number of detections / Number of hunting sessions.

Interpretation: A high number of detections may indicate effective hunting strategies or an evolving threat landscape. Conversely, a low detection rate could suggest the need for refinement in hunting techniques or a focus on different areas of the environment.

2.2 Mean Time to Detection (MTTD)

Description: MTTD measures the average time taken to detect threats during hunting activities. It is a critical metric for understanding the responsiveness of threat hunting efforts.

Calculation: Total time taken to detect threats / Total number of threats detected.

Interpretation: A lower MTTD indicates that threats are being identified quickly, which can minimize potential damage. Tracking this metric over time can reveal trends in detection speed and help identify areas for improvement.

2.3 Mean Time to Response (MTTR)

Description: MTTR gauges the average time taken to respond to threats once they have been detected. It reflects the efficiency of the incident response process.

Calculation: Total time taken to respond to threats / Total number of threats responded to.

Interpretation: A lower MTTR signifies a more effective incident response capability. This KPI can help teams evaluate their readiness to act on detected threats and may inform training needs or process adjustments.

2.4 Threat Remediation Rate

Description: This KPI measures the percentage of detected threats that are effectively remediated or resolved by the threat hunting team.

Calculation: (Number of threats remediated / Total number of detected threats) x 100.

Interpretation: A high remediation rate indicates that the threat hunting team is successfully addressing identified threats, while a low rate may suggest issues in the remediation process or a need for improved collaboration with incident response teams.

2.5 Hunting Session Frequency

Description: This KPI tracks how often threat hunting sessions are conducted over a specific period, reflecting the proactive nature of the security team.

Calculation: Total number of hunting sessions / Time period (e.g., weekly, monthly).

Interpretation: An increase in hunting session frequency can signify a heightened focus on proactive security measures and responsiveness to emerging threats.

3. Advanced KPIs for Threat Hunting

In addition to the essential KPIs, organizations may consider more advanced metrics to gain deeper insights into their threat hunting effectiveness:

3.1 Quality of Findings

Description: This KPI evaluates the quality and relevance of findings from threat hunts. It can be measured through post-hunt reviews and feedback from incident response teams.

Calculation: A qualitative assessment based on predefined criteria, such as accuracy, relevance, and actionable insights.

Interpretation: High-quality findings that lead to successful detections or remediations demonstrate effective hunting strategies. Poor quality may indicate the need for refining hunting techniques or further training for hunters.

3.2 Rate of False Positives

Description: This KPI tracks the percentage of identified threats that turn out to be false positives, indicating the accuracy of the threat hunting process.

Calculation: (Number of false positives / Total number of detections) x 100.

Interpretation: A low rate of false positives indicates that threat hunters are accurately identifying real threats. A high rate may suggest the need for improved criteria in detection or more refined hunting methods.

3.3 Threat Landscape Coverage

Description: This KPI assesses how well the threat hunting efforts cover the organization's critical assets, networks, and systems.

Calculation: Percentage of assets covered by threat hunting activities compared to the total number of critical assets.

Interpretation: A high coverage percentage suggests that the organization is proactive in identifying threats across its environment. Low coverage may highlight gaps in hunting efforts that need to be addressed.

4. Implementing and Monitoring KPIs

To effectively implement and monitor KPIs in threat hunting, organizations should follow these best practices:

4.1 Set Clear Objectives

Define specific objectives for each KPI that align with the organization's overall cybersecurity strategy. Ensure that these objectives are measurable and time-bound.

4.2 Automate Data Collection

Utilize security information and event management (SIEM) systems, threat intelligence platforms, and other automation tools to collect data for KPIs. Automation can help streamline the monitoring process and reduce manual effort.

4.3 Regularly Review and Adjust KPIs

Conduct regular reviews of KPIs to ensure they remain relevant and aligned with organizational goals. Adjust the metrics as necessary to reflect changes in the threat landscape or organizational priorities.

4.4 Report and Communicate Findings

Create regular reports to share KPI results with stakeholders, including management and security teams. Effective communication of these metrics helps demonstrate the value of threat hunting efforts and supports informed decision-making.

5. Case Study: Implementing KPIs in a Security Operations Center (SOC)

A mid-sized financial institution sought to improve its threat hunting capabilities by implementing KPIs. The organization's security operations center (SOC) was experiencing challenges in demonstrating the effectiveness of its threat hunting initiatives.

Actions Taken:

KPI Selection: The SOC team selected KPIs including MTTD, MTTR, threat remediation rate, and the rate of false positives to measure their performance effectively.

Automation of Data Collection: The organization implemented a SIEM solution to automate data collection and reporting for the selected KPIs.

Regular Reviews: The SOC established a quarterly review process to assess KPI performance, adjust objectives, and communicate findings to senior management.

Outcome:

As a result of implementing KPIs, the financial institution's SOC gained valuable insights into the effectiveness of its threat hunting efforts. The team observed a significant reduction in MTTD and MTTR, indicating improved responsiveness to threats. Additionally, the rate of false positives decreased, enhancing the accuracy of threat detection. The organization was able to demonstrate the value of its threat hunting initiatives, leading to increased support for ongoing investment in proactive cybersecurity measures.

Key Performance Indicators are essential for measuring the effectiveness of threat hunting activities. By selecting relevant KPIs, automating data collection, and regularly reviewing performance, organizations can gain valuable insights into their threat hunting efforts. These metrics not only inform decision-making but also help demonstrate the value of proactive threat hunting to stakeholders. As the cybersecurity landscape continues to evolve, leveraging KPIs will be critical for organizations aiming to stay ahead of adversaries and enhance their overall security posture.

10.2 Continuous Improvement and Optimization

In an ever-evolving cyber threat landscape, continuous improvement and optimization are crucial for maintaining an effective threat hunting program. Cyber adversaries constantly adapt their tactics, techniques, and procedures (TTPs), making it essential for security teams to regularly refine their strategies and practices. This chapter explores the principles of continuous improvement, the methods for optimizing threat hunting processes, and the role of feedback loops in enhancing overall performance.

1. The Importance of Continuous Improvement

Continuous improvement is a proactive approach aimed at enhancing processes, products, or services over time. In the context of threat hunting, it involves regularly evaluating and refining methodologies to increase effectiveness and efficiency. The importance of continuous improvement in threat hunting can be summarized as follows:

Adaptation to Evolving Threats: Cyber threats are dynamic; adversaries frequently change their approaches. Continuous improvement allows threat hunters to adapt their tactics and remain one step ahead.

Increased Effectiveness: Regularly evaluating and refining hunting strategies can lead to higher detection rates and more successful threat mitigations.

Resource Optimization: Continuous improvement helps identify inefficiencies in the threat hunting process, enabling better resource allocation and enhanced productivity.

Enhanced Collaboration: A culture of continuous improvement fosters collaboration and communication among teams, ensuring that insights from threat hunting are shared and integrated across the security organization.

2. Frameworks for Continuous Improvement

Several frameworks can guide organizations in implementing continuous improvement in threat hunting. Some of the most notable include:

2.1 The Plan-Do-Check-Act (PDCA) Cycle

The PDCA cycle is a widely used framework for continuous improvement that consists of four stages:

Plan: Identify areas for improvement, set objectives, and develop a plan to address them. This could involve refining hunting hypotheses, enhancing detection capabilities, or optimizing tools.

Do: Implement the plan. Conduct threat hunting activities according to the new strategies or techniques developed during the planning phase.

Check: Evaluate the effectiveness of the changes made. Analyze performance data, review KPIs, and gather feedback from team members to assess what worked and what didn't.

Act: Based on the evaluation, make necessary adjustments to the processes or strategies. If successful, standardize the changes and incorporate them into ongoing operations.

2.2 Lean and Agile Methodologies

Lean and Agile methodologies emphasize flexibility, responsiveness, and continuous feedback. These principles can be applied to threat hunting in the following ways:

Lean: Focus on eliminating waste and optimizing processes. This could mean streamlining workflows, reducing time spent on low-value activities, and ensuring that every action taken in the hunting process contributes to value creation.

Agile: Embrace iterative cycles of development and feedback. Threat hunters can conduct short, focused hunting sprints, followed by reviews to identify areas for improvement and adaptation.

3. Key Areas for Optimization

To enhance the effectiveness of threat hunting, organizations should consider optimizing the following key areas:

3.1 Threat Hunting Hypotheses

Review and Refine: Regularly evaluate the effectiveness of existing hunting hypotheses. Analyze the outcomes of hunts to determine whether the hypotheses were accurate and valuable.

Incorporate New Threat Intelligence: Integrate the latest threat intelligence into hypothesis development. Staying updated on emerging threats and TTPs allows hunters to formulate relevant and timely hypotheses.

Collaboration with Incident Response: Collaborate with incident response teams to gain insights from previous incidents. This collaboration can lead to the development of hypotheses that are more aligned with real-world threats.

3.2 Tools and Technologies

Evaluate Current Tools: Periodically assess the effectiveness of current threat hunting tools. Determine whether they meet the evolving needs of the organization and if any new tools should be integrated.

Automate Routine Tasks: Identify repetitive tasks that can be automated, such as data collection and analysis. Automation can free up threat hunters to focus on more complex investigations.

Integrate Threat Intelligence Platforms: Ensure that threat intelligence tools are effectively integrated into the hunting process, providing hunters with the most relevant and actionable intelligence available.

3.3 Data Analysis Techniques

Advanced Analytics: Explore advanced data analytics techniques, such as machine learning and behavioral analysis, to enhance detection capabilities. These techniques can help identify anomalies and patterns that traditional methods might miss.

Feedback Loops: Establish feedback loops to continuously gather insights from threat hunters on the effectiveness of data analysis techniques. This can lead to the refinement of analytical methodologies.

Cross-Team Collaboration: Encourage collaboration between threat hunters, data scientists, and analysts to leverage different perspectives and expertise in data analysis, fostering innovation in detection methods.

4. The Role of Feedback Loops

Feedback loops are integral to the continuous improvement process. They allow organizations to gather insights and learn from experiences, ultimately leading to more effective threat hunting practices. Key aspects of feedback loops include:

4.1 Post-Hunt Reviews

Conduct post-hunt reviews after each threat hunting session to analyze outcomes, document findings, and discuss successes and challenges. This practice encourages knowledge sharing and helps teams learn from each hunt.

4.2 Metrics and KPIs Analysis

Regularly analyze KPI results to identify trends and areas for improvement. Metrics such as MTTD, MTTR, and detection rates can provide valuable insights into the effectiveness of hunting activities.

4.3 Team Retrospectives

Implement regular retrospectives with the threat hunting team to discuss what worked well, what didn't, and what could be improved. This collaborative environment encourages open dialogue and can lead to innovative ideas for process enhancements.

5. Case Study: Continuous Improvement in a Large Enterprise Security Team

A large enterprise security team faced challenges in maintaining effective threat hunting practices due to a rapidly evolving threat landscape. Recognizing the need for continuous improvement, they adopted a structured approach:

Actions Taken:

PDCA Implementation: The team implemented the PDCA cycle to evaluate their hunting strategies continuously. They set clear objectives for each hunting cycle and reviewed outcomes regularly.

Regular Training Sessions: The organization invested in regular training sessions for threat hunters to keep them updated on new techniques and emerging threats.

Feedback Mechanisms: Established feedback mechanisms through post-hunt reviews and team retrospectives, allowing team members to share insights and identify areas for improvement.

Outcome:

As a result of these continuous improvement efforts, the enterprise security team significantly enhanced its threat hunting capabilities. They observed a measurable increase in detection rates and a reduction in MTTD. The team also reported greater morale and collaboration, as members felt empowered to contribute ideas and improvements. This structured approach to continuous improvement not only fortified their defenses but also fostered a culture of innovation within the security team.

Continuous improvement and optimization are essential for maintaining an effective threat hunting program. By adopting frameworks like PDCA, leveraging Lean and Agile methodologies, and focusing on key areas for optimization, organizations can enhance their threat hunting capabilities. Establishing feedback loops and regularly reviewing and refining hunting processes will ensure that teams stay responsive to the dynamic threat landscape. As adversaries continue to evolve, embracing a culture of continuous improvement will be critical for organizations seeking to stay ahead of threats and protect their assets effectively.

10.3 Training and Skill Development for Threat Hunters

As cyber threats become increasingly sophisticated, the demand for skilled threat hunters continues to grow. To stay effective in identifying, investigating, and mitigating potential threats, threat hunters must continually enhance their knowledge and skills. This chapter delves into the importance of training and skill development for threat hunters, the various training methodologies, and the key skills that aspiring and current threat hunters should cultivate.

1. The Importance of Training and Skill Development

Training and skill development are essential for several reasons:

Rapidly Evolving Threat Landscape: Cyber adversaries are constantly developing new tactics, techniques, and procedures (TTPs). Regular training ensures that threat hunters remain informed about the latest trends and can adapt their strategies accordingly.

Technological Advancements: The tools and technologies used in threat hunting are continually evolving. Ongoing training helps hunters keep pace with new tools, methodologies, and best practices.

Enhanced Job Performance: Well-trained threat hunters are more effective in their roles, leading to improved detection rates, faster response times, and ultimately a stronger security posture for the organization.

Career Advancement: For individual threat hunters, continuous learning and skill development can lead to career advancement opportunities, making them more competitive in the job market.

2. Key Skills for Threat Hunters

To be effective in their roles, threat hunters should develop a diverse skill set, including:

2.1 Technical Skills

Networking Knowledge: Understanding network protocols, architectures, and traffic patterns is essential for identifying abnormal behavior and potential threats.

Operating System Proficiency: Familiarity with various operating systems (Windows, Linux, macOS) helps hunters analyze system logs and detect malicious activities effectively.

Scripting and Automation: Knowledge of programming languages such as Python, PowerShell, or Bash enables threat hunters to automate tasks, create custom tools, and analyze data efficiently.

Threat Intelligence Analysis: The ability to analyze and interpret threat intelligence feeds helps hunters stay informed about emerging threats and adversaries.

2.2 Analytical Skills

Data Analysis: Strong analytical skills are crucial for evaluating large volumes of data, identifying patterns, and distinguishing between normal and suspicious activities.

Critical Thinking: Threat hunters must be able to think critically and creatively, approaching problems from various angles to uncover hidden threats.

Problem-Solving: Effective problem-solving skills are essential for navigating complex situations and identifying appropriate responses to potential threats.

2.3 Soft Skills

Communication: Threat hunters must be able to communicate findings clearly and concisely, both verbally and in writing. This skill is crucial for collaborating with team members and presenting findings to stakeholders.

Teamwork: Collaboration is key in threat hunting, as hunters often work alongside incident response teams, analysts, and other stakeholders to address security incidents.

Adaptability: The cyber threat landscape is dynamic, and threat hunters must be willing to adapt their strategies and techniques in response to changing conditions.

3. Training Methodologies

Organizations should adopt various training methodologies to ensure comprehensive skill development for threat hunters:

3.1 Formal Training Programs

Certification Courses: Enroll threat hunters in industry-recognized certification programs, such as Certified Information Systems Security Professional (CISSP), Certified

Ethical Hacker (CEH), or GIAC Cyber Threat Intelligence (GCTI). These courses provide structured learning and credibility in the field.

Workshops and Boot Camps: Attend workshops and boot camps that focus on specific skills or tools. These intensive sessions often provide hands-on experience and practical insights.

3.2 On-the-Job Training

Mentorship Programs: Pair less experienced threat hunters with seasoned professionals for mentorship. This relationship allows for knowledge transfer and guidance on best practices in threat hunting.

Shadowing Opportunities: Encourage junior hunters to shadow senior colleagues during threat hunting activities. Observing real-world scenarios provides valuable context and understanding.

3.3 Self-Directed Learning

Online Resources: Utilize online courses, webinars, and tutorials to enable self-directed learning. Platforms like Coursera, Udemy, and Cybrary offer a wealth of content related to cybersecurity and threat hunting.

Reading and Research: Encourage threat hunters to stay updated on industry trends by reading blogs, white papers, and research reports from reputable sources. Staying informed about emerging threats and security practices is essential.

4. Building a Culture of Continuous Learning

Organizations should foster a culture of continuous learning and improvement in threat hunting. Here are several strategies to promote such a culture:

4.1 Regular Training Sessions

Conduct regular training sessions on relevant topics, including new tools, techniques, and emerging threats. These sessions can be in the form of lunch-and-learns, workshops, or guest speakers.

4.2 Encouragement of Certifications

Support threat hunters in pursuing certifications by offering financial assistance, study materials, or time off to prepare for exams. This support can motivate employees to enhance their skills and knowledge.

4.3 Knowledge Sharing

Create platforms for knowledge sharing, such as internal forums, wikis, or chat groups, where team members can exchange insights, tips, and resources related to threat hunting.

4.4 Performance Reviews and Feedback

Incorporate training and skill development into performance reviews. Provide constructive feedback to threat hunters, highlighting areas for improvement and offering opportunities for further training.

5. Case Study: Building a Training Program for a Security Operations Center (SOC)

A medium-sized organization recognized the need to enhance the skills of its threat hunting team to improve overall security posture. They decided to implement a structured training program.

Actions Taken:

Needs Assessment: Conducted a skills gap analysis to identify areas where team members needed improvement. This assessment informed the training program's development.

Diverse Training Methods: Developed a training program that included formal certification courses, hands-on workshops, and self-directed learning opportunities.

Mentorship Program: Established a mentorship program that paired junior threat hunters with experienced mentors for guidance and support.

Outcome:

The implementation of the training program resulted in significant improvements in the team's threat hunting capabilities. The threat hunting team reported higher confidence in their skills and increased effectiveness in detecting and responding to threats.

Additionally, the organization benefited from a stronger security posture, with reduced incident response times and improved collaboration among security teams.

Training and skill development are critical components of an effective threat hunting program. By cultivating a diverse skill set and utilizing various training methodologies, organizations can ensure that their threat hunters are well-equipped to tackle evolving cyber threats. Fostering a culture of continuous learning and improvement will further enhance the effectiveness of threat hunting efforts, ultimately contributing to a stronger overall security posture. As the cyber threat landscape continues to evolve, investing in the development of threat hunting skills is essential for organizations seeking to stay ahead of adversaries and protect their assets effectively.

11. Legal, Ethical, and Compliance Considerations

As organizations engage in proactive cyber threat hunting, navigating the complex landscape of legal, ethical, and compliance considerations becomes paramount. In this chapter, we will explore the various legal frameworks and regulations that govern cybersecurity practices, including data protection laws, privacy regulations, and industry-specific compliance standards. We will discuss the implications of these laws on threat hunting activities, highlighting the need for organizations to ensure that their practices align with legal requirements while maintaining ethical boundaries. Furthermore, we will examine the importance of transparency and accountability in threat hunting efforts, emphasizing how ethical considerations impact the trust and confidence of stakeholders. By understanding and addressing the legal and ethical implications of threat hunting, organizations can create a responsible and compliant cybersecurity strategy that not only protects their assets but also respects the rights and privacy of individuals.

11.1 Privacy and Compliance in Threat Hunting

As cyber threats continue to grow in sophistication and frequency, organizations increasingly rely on threat hunting to proactively identify and mitigate risks. However, the nature of threat hunting often involves monitoring user activity, analyzing data, and accessing sensitive information, which raises significant privacy and compliance concerns. This chapter explores the interplay between privacy and compliance in threat hunting, highlighting key considerations, regulations, and best practices to ensure that organizations navigate this complex landscape effectively.

1. The Importance of Privacy and Compliance

Privacy and compliance are critical in threat hunting for several reasons:

Legal Obligations: Organizations are subject to various laws and regulations governing data protection and privacy, such as the General Data Protection Regulation (GDPR), the Health Insurance Portability and Accountability Act (HIPAA), and the California Consumer Privacy Act (CCPA). Non-compliance can result in severe financial penalties and reputational damage.

Trust and Reputation: Organizations that respect user privacy and comply with regulations build trust with their customers and stakeholders. Demonstrating a commitment to ethical practices can enhance an organization's reputation in the marketplace.

Risk Mitigation: Privacy violations can lead to data breaches, resulting in legal liabilities, financial losses, and damage to customer relationships. A robust privacy and compliance strategy helps mitigate these risks.

2. Key Privacy Regulations and Frameworks

Several key regulations and frameworks influence privacy practices in threat hunting. Understanding these regulations is essential for compliance:

2.1 General Data Protection Regulation (GDPR)

The GDPR is a comprehensive data protection law in the European Union that governs the processing of personal data. Key principles include:

Lawful Basis for Processing: Organizations must have a valid legal basis for processing personal data, such as consent or legitimate interests.

Data Minimization: Only the minimum amount of personal data necessary for a specific purpose should be collected and processed.

Transparency: Organizations must inform individuals about how their data is collected, processed, and stored.

Rights of Individuals: Individuals have rights regarding their data, including the right to access, rectify, and erase their personal information.

2.2 Health Insurance Portability and Accountability Act (HIPAA)

For organizations in the healthcare sector, HIPAA sets standards for protecting sensitive patient information. Key components include:

Protected Health Information (PHI): Organizations must implement safeguards to protect PHI from unauthorized access or disclosure.

Breach Notification: In the event of a data breach involving PHI, organizations must notify affected individuals and regulatory authorities promptly.

2.3 California Consumer Privacy Act (CCPA)

The CCPA enhances privacy rights for California residents. Key provisions include:

Consumer Rights: Consumers have the right to know what personal data is being collected, the right to access their data, and the right to request deletion.

Business Obligations: Businesses must disclose their data collection practices and allow consumers to opt out of the sale of their personal information.

3. Privacy Considerations in Threat Hunting

While threat hunting is essential for identifying and mitigating risks, it often involves sensitive data that requires careful handling. Key privacy considerations include:

3.1 Data Collection Practices

Purpose Limitation: Ensure that data collection is limited to what is necessary for threat hunting activities. Avoid collecting data that is unrelated to the hunting process.

Anonymization and Pseudonymization: Where possible, anonymize or pseudonymize data to protect individual identities. This approach reduces the risk of privacy violations.

Informed Consent: When collecting personal data, obtain informed consent from individuals where required by law. Clearly communicate the purpose and scope of data collection.

3.2 Monitoring and Surveillance

Transparency: Be transparent with employees and users about monitoring practices. Provide clear information about what data is being collected, how it will be used, and who will have access to it.

Employee Training: Train employees on privacy policies and compliance requirements to ensure they understand the importance of privacy in threat hunting.

Policy Enforcement: Establish policies governing monitoring and surveillance activities, including guidelines on how data should be handled and stored.

3.3 Incident Response and Data Breaches

Breach Response Plan: Develop and implement a breach response plan that outlines steps to take in the event of a data breach. This plan should include notification protocols and remedial actions.

Regular Audits: Conduct regular audits of data handling practices to ensure compliance with privacy regulations and identify areas for improvement.

4. Balancing Security and Privacy

Striking a balance between effective threat hunting and protecting individual privacy is a significant challenge for organizations. Here are some strategies to achieve this balance:

4.1 Risk Assessment

Conduct thorough risk assessments to identify potential privacy risks associated with threat hunting activities. Understanding the risks helps organizations make informed decisions about data collection and monitoring practices.

4.2 Privacy by Design

Incorporate privacy considerations into the design and implementation of threat hunting programs. This proactive approach ensures that privacy is embedded in all processes and technologies used for hunting.

4.3 Collaboration with Legal and Compliance Teams

Engage legal and compliance teams early in the threat hunting process to ensure that activities align with regulatory requirements. Collaboration ensures that hunting practices do not inadvertently violate privacy laws.

5. Best Practices for Privacy and Compliance in Threat Hunting

Organizations can adopt several best practices to enhance privacy and compliance in their threat hunting efforts:

5.1 Develop Comprehensive Policies

Create and implement comprehensive privacy policies that outline data collection, usage, and handling practices related to threat hunting. Ensure that these policies are regularly reviewed and updated to reflect changing regulations.

5.2 Conduct Regular Training

Provide regular training for threat hunters and security teams on privacy regulations, compliance requirements, and ethical considerations. Ensuring that all team members are aware of their responsibilities helps minimize privacy risks.

5.3 Establish Governance Frameworks

Establish governance frameworks to oversee data handling practices in threat hunting. This framework should include designated personnel responsible for privacy compliance and regular oversight.

5.4 Utilize Privacy-Enhancing Technologies

Leverage privacy-enhancing technologies (PETs) to facilitate compliance with privacy regulations. These technologies can help automate data protection measures and reduce the risk of privacy violations.

Privacy and compliance are integral components of effective threat hunting. Organizations must navigate a complex landscape of regulations while ensuring that their threat hunting activities do not infringe on individual privacy rights. By understanding key privacy regulations, implementing best practices, and fostering a culture of compliance, organizations can effectively balance security needs with privacy considerations. As the cyber threat landscape continues to evolve, maintaining a commitment to privacy and compliance will be crucial for building trust, mitigating risks, and safeguarding sensitive information.

11.2 Ethical Boundaries in Cyber Threat Hunting

As organizations increasingly adopt proactive measures like threat hunting to combat cyber threats, ethical considerations become paramount. Cyber threat hunting involves monitoring systems, analyzing user behavior, and gathering intelligence to identify potential threats, which can raise significant ethical concerns. This chapter explores the ethical boundaries in cyber threat hunting, highlighting the responsibilities of threat hunters, potential ethical dilemmas, and best practices to maintain ethical standards.

1. The Ethical Imperative in Cyber Threat Hunting

Ethics play a critical role in threat hunting for several reasons:

Trust: Organizations must maintain the trust of their employees, customers, and stakeholders. Ethical practices in threat hunting foster a sense of trust and transparency regarding how data is collected, analyzed, and utilized.

Legal Compliance: Ethical conduct often aligns with legal requirements. Adhering to ethical standards can help organizations avoid legal pitfalls and reputational damage.

Accountability: Ethical guidelines promote accountability among threat hunters, ensuring that they act responsibly and in the organization's best interest.

2. Defining Ethical Boundaries in Threat Hunting

To navigate the ethical landscape of threat hunting, organizations should establish clear boundaries that guide the actions of threat hunters. Key considerations include:

2.1 Transparency and Disclosure

Informed Consent: Organizations should obtain informed consent from employees regarding monitoring practices. Clear communication about what data will be collected, how it will be used, and who will have access to it is crucial.

Open Communication: Establish open channels of communication with employees to address concerns about monitoring and data collection. Transparency helps build trust and alleviates fears of surveillance.

2.2 Purpose Limitation

Specific Objectives: Threat hunting should have clearly defined objectives that align with the organization's security goals. The purpose of monitoring and data collection should be communicated to all stakeholders.

Data Minimization: Collect only the data necessary to achieve the objectives of threat hunting. Avoid collecting excessive or irrelevant information that could infringe on individuals' privacy.

2.3 Non-Discrimination and Fairness

Equality in Monitoring: Ensure that monitoring practices are applied consistently and fairly across all employees. Avoid targeting specific individuals or groups without justifiable cause.

Avoiding Bias: Be aware of potential biases in data analysis and decision-making processes. Threat hunters should strive to approach investigations objectively, minimizing the risk of discriminatory practices.

3. Ethical Dilemmas in Threat Hunting

Despite clear ethical boundaries, threat hunters may encounter various ethical dilemmas. Some common dilemmas include:

3.1 Privacy vs. Security

Conflict of Interest: Threat hunters often face the challenge of balancing privacy rights with the need for security. Striking this balance requires careful consideration of how much monitoring is necessary to protect the organization without infringing on individual privacy.

Surveillance Overreach: Overzealous monitoring can lead to a culture of mistrust and anxiety among employees. Threat hunters must be mindful of how their actions may impact workplace morale and individual privacy.

3.2 Data Handling and Ownership

Data Ownership: Ethical questions arise regarding the ownership of data collected during threat hunting. Organizations must clarify who owns the data and how it will be used, ensuring transparency in data handling practices.

Retention Policies: Establishing data retention policies is essential to avoid retaining data longer than necessary. Ethical dilemmas may arise if data is kept indefinitely, especially when it contains sensitive information.

3.3 Disclosures and Reporting

Responsible Disclosure: Threat hunters may discover vulnerabilities or security issues during their investigations. Ethical considerations arise regarding how to disclose these findings responsibly, both within the organization and to external stakeholders.

Reporting Misconduct: If threat hunters uncover unethical behavior within the organization, they face the ethical dilemma of whether to report it. Balancing loyalty to the organization with the responsibility to uphold ethical standards can be challenging.

4. Best Practices for Maintaining Ethical Standards

Organizations can implement several best practices to uphold ethical standards in threat hunting:

4.1 Establish an Ethical Framework

Code of Ethics: Develop a comprehensive code of ethics that outlines the organization's commitment to ethical behavior in threat hunting. This framework should guide decision-making processes and set expectations for conduct.

Regular Training: Provide regular training on ethical considerations in threat hunting for all team members. Ongoing education helps reinforce ethical principles and keeps staff informed about best practices.

4.2 Foster a Culture of Ethics

Encourage Open Dialogue: Create an environment where employees feel comfortable discussing ethical concerns and dilemmas. Encourage open dialogue to address potential issues proactively.

Empower Employees: Empower threat hunters to raise concerns about unethical practices or dilemmas they encounter. Providing avenues for reporting can help organizations address issues before they escalate.

4.3 Engage Legal and Compliance Teams

Collaboration with Legal Counsel: Involve legal and compliance teams in the development of threat hunting policies and practices. Their expertise can help ensure that ethical considerations align with legal requirements.

Policy Reviews: Conduct regular reviews of threat hunting policies to ensure they remain compliant with ethical standards and legal obligations.

5. Case Study: Implementing Ethical Practices in Threat Hunting

An organization in the finance sector recognized the need for ethical practices in its threat hunting efforts due to the sensitive nature of its data. They took the following steps:

Actions Taken:

Developed a Code of Ethics: The organization created a code of ethics that emphasized transparency, data minimization, and fair treatment of employees. This code served as a guiding document for threat hunters.

Established a Reporting Mechanism: They implemented a reporting mechanism for employees to raise ethical concerns without fear of retaliation. This process encouraged accountability and open communication.

Conducted Regular Training: The organization provided ongoing training sessions on ethical considerations and legal compliance in threat hunting, reinforcing the importance of ethical behavior.

Outcome:

The implementation of ethical practices in threat hunting resulted in improved trust among employees and a stronger security posture for the organization. Employees felt more comfortable reporting potential issues, leading to proactive identification and resolution of vulnerabilities. The organization was able to navigate complex ethical dilemmas while maintaining a commitment to security and privacy.

Ethical boundaries in cyber threat hunting are essential for maintaining trust, accountability, and compliance within organizations. By establishing clear ethical guidelines, fostering a culture of ethics, and addressing potential dilemmas, organizations can navigate the complex landscape of threat hunting responsibly. As the cyber threat landscape continues to evolve, a commitment to ethical practices will be vital for ensuring that threat hunting efforts enhance security without compromising individual rights or organizational integrity.

11.3 Legal Implications of Threat Intelligence Sharing

In the realm of cybersecurity, sharing threat intelligence is increasingly recognized as a critical component of an effective defense strategy. By exchanging information about potential threats, vulnerabilities, and incidents, organizations can enhance their situational awareness and improve their ability to respond to cyber threats. However, sharing threat intelligence also raises a host of legal implications that organizations must navigate carefully. This chapter delves into the legal landscape surrounding threat intelligence sharing, focusing on relevant laws, regulations, risks, and best practices to mitigate legal liabilities.

1. The Importance of Threat Intelligence Sharing

Threat intelligence sharing allows organizations to benefit from collective knowledge, improving their security posture and enhancing their ability to detect and respond to threats. The benefits include:

Improved Detection and Response: Sharing information about indicators of compromise (IOCs) and tactics, techniques, and procedures (TTPs) enables organizations to identify threats more effectively.

Collective Defense: Organizations can collaborate to defend against common adversaries, creating a more resilient security ecosystem.

Legal and Regulatory Compliance: In some sectors, sharing threat intelligence can be necessary for compliance with legal and regulatory requirements.

2. Legal Frameworks Governing Threat Intelligence Sharing

The legal implications of threat intelligence sharing are influenced by various laws and regulations. Understanding these frameworks is essential for organizations engaged in intelligence sharing:

2.1 Data Protection and Privacy Laws

General Data Protection Regulation (GDPR): In the European Union, the GDPR imposes strict rules on the processing of personal data. Organizations must ensure that any shared threat intelligence complies with GDPR requirements, particularly concerning data minimization, lawful processing, and individuals' rights.

Health Insurance Portability and Accountability Act (HIPAA): In the healthcare sector, HIPAA governs the protection of protected health information (PHI). Organizations must be cautious when sharing threat intelligence that may contain PHI, as unauthorized disclosures can lead to significant penalties.

California Consumer Privacy Act (CCPA): The CCPA provides California residents with certain rights regarding their personal information. Organizations must ensure that any shared intelligence complies with these rights, particularly concerning consent and data sharing practices.

2.2 Intellectual Property Laws

Trade Secrets: Threat intelligence may contain proprietary information or trade secrets. Sharing such information without proper legal safeguards can expose organizations to legal risks and potential intellectual property theft.

Licensing Agreements: When utilizing third-party threat intelligence services, organizations should carefully review licensing agreements to understand their rights and obligations regarding sharing and using the intelligence.

2.3 Anti-Trust and Competition Laws

Collusion Risks: Sharing threat intelligence among competitors can raise anti-trust concerns. Organizations must be cautious to avoid any appearance of collusion or price-fixing, which could result in legal scrutiny.

Safe Harbors: Some jurisdictions provide legal safe harbors for organizations that engage in collaborative information sharing for cybersecurity purposes, but organizations must ensure they meet specific criteria to qualify for such protections.

3. Risks Associated with Threat Intelligence Sharing

Engaging in threat intelligence sharing carries inherent risks that organizations must manage:

3.1 Data Breaches and Unauthorized Access

Sensitive Information Exposure: Sharing threat intelligence may inadvertently expose sensitive information, leading to potential data breaches or unauthorized access.

Liability for Breaches: If shared intelligence results in a data breach for another organization, the sharing entity may face legal liability, especially if negligence in sharing practices is demonstrated.

3.2 Misuse of Shared Intelligence

Inappropriate Use: There is a risk that shared threat intelligence may be misused by recipients, leading to reputational damage or legal repercussions for the original sharing organization.

Accountability: Organizations must establish clear guidelines and agreements regarding how shared intelligence can be used to mitigate the risk of misuse.

3.3 Compliance Failures

Regulatory Scrutiny: Failure to comply with relevant data protection and privacy laws can result in significant fines and legal challenges, particularly for organizations that share intelligence without adequate safeguards.

Reputational Damage: Legal issues arising from improper sharing practices can lead to reputational damage, undermining stakeholder trust and confidence.

4. Best Practices for Legal Compliance in Threat Intelligence Sharing

To mitigate legal risks associated with threat intelligence sharing, organizations can adopt several best practices:

4.1 Establish Clear Policies and Procedures

Data Classification: Develop policies for classifying and categorizing threat intelligence based on sensitivity and legal implications. This classification helps determine what can be shared and under what conditions.

Information Sharing Agreements: Use formal agreements to outline the terms and conditions of sharing threat intelligence. These agreements should clarify the responsibilities of each party, usage rights, and liability limitations.

4.2 Conduct Risk Assessments

Legal and Compliance Reviews: Before sharing threat intelligence, conduct thorough legal and compliance reviews to identify potential risks and ensure adherence to applicable laws and regulations.

Risk Mitigation Strategies: Develop strategies to mitigate identified risks, including data anonymization, encryption, and limited sharing of sensitive information.

4.3 Engage Legal Counsel

Legal Consultation: Involve legal counsel when developing threat intelligence sharing policies and practices. Legal experts can provide guidance on compliance requirements and potential liabilities.

Ongoing Monitoring of Regulations: Stay informed about evolving legal and regulatory frameworks related to data protection, privacy, and cybersecurity. Regular updates help organizations adapt their practices to changing requirements.

The legal implications of threat intelligence sharing are multifaceted and require careful consideration by organizations. While sharing threat intelligence is essential for enhancing cybersecurity resilience, it must be approached with a clear understanding of applicable laws and regulations. By establishing robust policies, conducting risk assessments, and engaging legal counsel, organizations can navigate the complexities of threat intelligence sharing while minimizing legal liabilities. As cyber threats continue to evolve, a proactive and legally compliant approach to intelligence sharing will be crucial for fostering collaboration and enhancing collective defense in the cybersecurity landscape.

12. Future of Cyber Threat Hunting

As the digital landscape continues to evolve, the future of cyber threat hunting promises to be both challenging and exciting, driven by emerging technologies and the ever-changing tactics of adversaries. In this chapter, we will explore the anticipated trends and innovations that will shape the field of threat hunting in the coming years. We will discuss the increasing role of artificial intelligence and machine learning in automating detection processes, enhancing analysis capabilities, and improving threat prediction. Additionally, we will examine the growing significance of cloud security and the challenges it presents for threat hunters in a multi-cloud environment. The chapter will also address the need for advanced skills and continuous learning, emphasizing the importance of adapting to new tools and methodologies as the threat landscape evolves. By preparing for these changes and embracing innovative approaches, organizations can stay ahead of cyber adversaries, ensuring their threat hunting efforts remain effective and relevant in a dynamic cybersecurity landscape.

12.1 Emerging Technologies in Threat Hunting

The landscape of cybersecurity is rapidly evolving, driven by the increasing sophistication of cyber threats and the corresponding need for advanced threat hunting techniques. As organizations strive to stay ahead of adversaries, emerging technologies play a pivotal role in enhancing threat hunting capabilities. This chapter explores the latest technological advancements that are shaping the future of threat hunting, highlighting how these innovations can empower organizations to detect, respond to, and mitigate cyber threats more effectively.

1. The Role of Technology in Threat Hunting

Threat hunting involves proactively searching for indicators of compromise (IOCs) and threats that may evade traditional security measures. Technology is at the core of this process, enabling threat hunters to analyze vast amounts of data, automate repetitive tasks, and leverage advanced analytical techniques. Key technological advancements in threat hunting include:

Artificial Intelligence (AI) and Machine Learning (ML): These technologies are transforming the threat hunting landscape by enabling automated detection of anomalies and patterns indicative of malicious activities. AI and ML algorithms can analyze large datasets quickly, providing threat hunters with actionable insights.

Big Data Analytics: The ability to process and analyze massive volumes of data from diverse sources is crucial for effective threat hunting. Big data analytics tools enable threat hunters to identify trends and correlations that may indicate potential threats.

Threat Intelligence Platforms (TIPs): TIPs aggregate and analyze threat intelligence data from multiple sources, providing organizations with a comprehensive view of the threat landscape. These platforms facilitate information sharing and collaboration among threat hunters, enhancing their ability to identify and respond to emerging threats.

2. Key Emerging Technologies in Threat Hunting

2.1 Extended Detection and Response (XDR)

Extended Detection and Response (XDR) is an advanced security solution that integrates data from various security tools and platforms to provide a holistic view of an organization's security posture. Key features of XDR include:

Unified Data Collection: XDR collects and correlates data from endpoints, servers, networks, and cloud environments, providing threat hunters with a comprehensive view of the threat landscape.

Automated Response Capabilities: XDR solutions often include automated response capabilities, enabling organizations to swiftly contain and remediate threats without human intervention.

Enhanced Analytics: XDR leverages machine learning and behavioral analytics to detect sophisticated threats that may go unnoticed by traditional security tools.

2.2 Security Orchestration, Automation, and Response (SOAR)

Security Orchestration, Automation, and Response (SOAR) platforms enable organizations to automate security operations and streamline incident response. Key benefits of SOAR in threat hunting include:

Workflow Automation: SOAR platforms automate repetitive tasks, allowing threat hunters to focus on more complex investigations and reducing response times.

Integration of Security Tools: SOAR facilitates integration between disparate security tools, enabling seamless data sharing and enhancing overall security effectiveness.

Incident Response Playbooks: SOAR platforms provide predefined incident response playbooks that guide threat hunters through standardized response procedures, ensuring consistency and efficiency in threat mitigation.

2.3 Threat Hunting as a Service (THaaS)

Threat Hunting as a Service (THaaS) is an emerging model where organizations outsource their threat hunting efforts to specialized service providers. This approach offers several advantages:

Access to Expertise: THaaS providers bring specialized knowledge and experience in threat hunting, allowing organizations to leverage their expertise without needing to build an in-house team.

Scalability: Organizations can scale their threat hunting capabilities up or down based on their evolving needs, providing flexibility in resource allocation.

Cost-Effectiveness: Outsourcing threat hunting can be more cost-effective than maintaining a dedicated team, particularly for smaller organizations with limited budgets.

3. Advanced Analytical Techniques

Emerging technologies also encompass advanced analytical techniques that enhance threat hunting capabilities. Key techniques include:

3.1 Behavioral Analytics

Behavioral analytics involves monitoring user and entity behavior to identify anomalies that may indicate malicious activities. Key aspects of behavioral analytics include:

Establishing Baselines: Organizations establish normal behavior baselines for users and systems, enabling the detection of deviations that may signal potential threats.

User and Entity Behavior Analytics (UEBA): UEBA solutions leverage machine learning to analyze patterns of behavior across users and entities, providing threat hunters with insights into unusual activities.

3.2 Threat Emulation and Red Teaming

Threat emulation and red teaming involve simulating real-world attacks to identify vulnerabilities and weaknesses in an organization's security posture. Key components include:

Adversarial Simulation: Red teams simulate tactics, techniques, and procedures (TTPs) used by real-world adversaries to assess an organization's defenses.

Continuous Testing: Regular red teaming exercises provide organizations with ongoing assessments of their security effectiveness, enabling proactive identification and remediation of vulnerabilities.

4. The Impact of Cloud Technologies

The shift to cloud-based environments presents new challenges and opportunities for threat hunting. Key impacts of cloud technologies include:

4.1 Cloud Security Posture Management (CSPM)

CSPM tools enable organizations to monitor and manage their cloud security posture, helping to identify misconfigurations and compliance violations. Key benefits include:

Visibility Across Cloud Environments: CSPM provides visibility into cloud assets and configurations, allowing threat hunters to identify potential vulnerabilities.

Automated Compliance Checks: CSPM solutions automate compliance checks against industry standards, ensuring that organizations maintain a secure cloud environment.

4.2 Container Security

As organizations increasingly adopt containerization, securing containerized applications becomes essential. Key considerations for container security include:

Runtime Protection: Implementing runtime protection for containers helps detect and respond to threats in real-time.

Image Scanning: Scanning container images for vulnerabilities before deployment mitigates the risk of deploying insecure applications.

Emerging technologies are reshaping the threat hunting landscape, enabling organizations to adopt more proactive and sophisticated approaches to cybersecurity. By leveraging advancements such as XDR, SOAR, behavioral analytics, and cloud security solutions, organizations can enhance their threat hunting capabilities and improve their overall security posture. As the threat landscape continues to evolve, staying abreast of emerging technologies will be critical for organizations seeking to effectively combat cyber threats and safeguard their digital assets. Embracing these innovations will empower threat hunters to identify and mitigate threats more efficiently, ultimately contributing to a more resilient cybersecurity ecosystem.

12.2 Adapting to New and Evolving Threats

In the rapidly changing landscape of cybersecurity, organizations face an ongoing battle against a diverse array of threats that are constantly evolving in complexity and sophistication. As attackers leverage new technologies and tactics, threat hunters must adapt their strategies and methodologies to effectively identify and mitigate these emerging risks. This chapter explores the key principles and practices organizations can adopt to stay ahead of new and evolving threats, ensuring a proactive approach to cybersecurity.

1. The Dynamic Nature of Cyber Threats

Cyber threats are not static; they evolve in response to technological advancements, changes in user behavior, and shifts in the threat landscape. Key factors contributing to this dynamism include:

Emergence of Advanced Persistent Threats (APTs): APTs are sophisticated, targeted attacks often carried out by well-funded adversaries. These threats employ a range of tactics, techniques, and procedures (TTPs) to infiltrate networks and remain undetected for extended periods.

Rise of Ransomware: Ransomware attacks have become increasingly prevalent, with attackers employing tactics such as double extortion, where they not only encrypt data but also threaten to leak sensitive information.

Exploitation of Remote Work: The shift to remote work has expanded the attack surface, creating new vulnerabilities as employees access corporate resources from unsecured environments.

2. Principles for Adapting to Evolving Threats

To effectively combat new and evolving threats, organizations should adopt the following principles:

2.1 Continuous Threat Assessment

Regular Threat Intelligence Updates: Organizations must continually gather and analyze threat intelligence to stay informed about emerging threats and attack vectors. This involves subscribing to threat intelligence feeds, participating in information-sharing communities, and monitoring industry reports.

Vulnerability Management: Implement a robust vulnerability management program that regularly assesses systems for weaknesses and ensures timely patching and remediation of identified vulnerabilities.

2.2 Flexibility in Security Posture

Agile Security Frameworks: Adopt agile security frameworks that allow for rapid adjustments to security policies, procedures, and technologies in response to changing threats. This includes embracing methodologies like DevSecOps, where security practices are integrated into the development lifecycle.

Dynamic Threat Models: Develop and maintain dynamic threat models that reflect the current threat landscape, enabling organizations to prioritize security efforts based on the most relevant risks.

2.3 Enhanced Detection Capabilities

Behavioral Analytics: Leverage behavioral analytics to detect anomalies indicative of emerging threats. By establishing baselines of normal behavior, organizations can quickly identify deviations that may signal malicious activities.

Machine Learning and AI: Implement machine learning and artificial intelligence (AI) solutions to enhance threat detection capabilities. These technologies can analyze large volumes of data and identify patterns indicative of new threats more effectively than traditional methods.

3. Strategies for Proactive Threat Hunting

To stay ahead of emerging threats, organizations should implement proactive threat hunting strategies that focus on identifying and mitigating risks before they result in incidents:

3.1 Threat Simulation Exercises

Red Teaming: Conduct regular red teaming exercises to simulate real-world attacks and assess the organization's defenses. These exercises help identify vulnerabilities and provide insights into the tactics used by adversaries.

Tabletop Exercises: Organize tabletop exercises that bring together stakeholders to discuss and evaluate responses to hypothetical threat scenarios. These exercises foster collaboration and improve incident response capabilities.

3.2 Investing in Threat Intelligence Platforms

Integration of Threat Intelligence: Utilize threat intelligence platforms that aggregate data from various sources, providing comprehensive insights into the threat landscape. This information can inform threat hunting efforts and enhance situational awareness.

Collaborative Threat Intelligence Sharing: Participate in information-sharing communities to exchange threat intelligence with peers and industry partners. Collaborative efforts can improve detection capabilities and foster a collective defense against common adversaries.

4. Embracing Emerging Technologies

Organizations should leverage emerging technologies to enhance their threat hunting capabilities and adapt to evolving threats effectively:

4.1 Automation and Orchestration

Security Automation: Implement security automation to streamline threat hunting processes, reducing response times and allowing threat hunters to focus on more complex investigations. Automated tools can also assist in data collection and analysis.

Security Orchestration: Use security orchestration platforms to integrate and automate workflows across multiple security tools, improving efficiency and effectiveness in threat detection and response.

4.2 Cloud Security Solutions

Cloud Threat Hunting: As organizations increasingly adopt cloud services, implementing cloud security solutions becomes essential for threat hunting. This includes monitoring cloud environments for anomalous activities and vulnerabilities.

Zero Trust Architecture: Adopt a zero trust approach that assumes threats could be present both outside and within the network. This framework involves continuously verifying user identities and device trustworthiness, minimizing the potential impact of attacks.

5. Building a Resilient Security Culture

To effectively adapt to new and evolving threats, organizations must cultivate a security-conscious culture among employees:

5.1 Security Awareness Training

Regular Training Programs: Implement ongoing security awareness training programs to educate employees about emerging threats, phishing tactics, and safe online practices. A well-informed workforce can serve as an additional layer of defense against cyber threats.

Incident Reporting Culture: Encourage a culture of incident reporting, where employees feel empowered to report suspicious activities without fear of reprisal. This can lead to quicker identification and response to potential threats.

5.2 Cross-Functional Collaboration

Interdepartmental Cooperation: Foster collaboration between IT, security, and business units to enhance threat hunting efforts. Cross-functional teams can share insights and improve overall security posture.

Engagement with External Partners: Collaborate with external partners, such as managed security service providers (MSSPs) and threat intelligence firms, to augment internal capabilities and gain access to specialized knowledge.

Adapting to new and evolving threats requires a proactive and multifaceted approach to cybersecurity. By implementing continuous threat assessment practices, enhancing detection capabilities, investing in emerging technologies, and fostering a security-conscious culture, organizations can effectively stay ahead of adversaries. As the threat landscape continues to evolve, organizations that embrace flexibility and agility in their security strategies will be better positioned to mitigate risks and protect their digital assets. In this dynamic environment, the ability to adapt and innovate will be critical to ensuring resilience against future cyber threats.

12.3 The Future Skills of a Threat Hunter

As the cybersecurity landscape becomes increasingly complex and adversaries employ sophisticated tactics, the role of the threat hunter is evolving rapidly. To effectively combat emerging threats, future threat hunters must develop a diverse set of skills that blend technical knowledge, analytical thinking, and interpersonal capabilities. This chapter explores the essential skills that will define the next generation of threat hunters, ensuring they are equipped to meet the challenges of a dynamic cyber threat landscape.

1. The Evolving Role of Threat Hunters

Traditionally, threat hunters focused primarily on identifying and responding to known threats within an organization's infrastructure. However, as cyber threats grow in sophistication, threat hunters must adapt their skill sets to encompass a broader range of responsibilities, including:

Proactive Threat Detection: Rather than solely reacting to incidents, future threat hunters will need to anticipate and identify potential threats before they manifest into real-world attacks.

Collaboration Across Teams: Effective threat hunting will increasingly require collaboration with various departments, including incident response, IT operations, and executive management.

Understanding of Business Context: Threat hunters must align their efforts with the organization's goals and risk appetite, ensuring that cybersecurity strategies support overall business objectives.

2. Key Skills for Future Threat Hunters

To excel in this evolving role, threat hunters must cultivate a range of skills across several domains:

2.1 Technical Skills

Advanced Malware Analysis: Threat hunters will need a deep understanding of malware analysis techniques, including static and dynamic analysis. This expertise enables them to dissect malicious code and understand its behavior, tactics, and impact on the organization.

Network and Endpoint Forensics: Proficiency in network traffic analysis and endpoint forensics is essential for identifying anomalies and indicators of compromise (IOCs). Future threat hunters should be skilled in using forensic tools to investigate incidents and gather evidence.

Scripting and Automation: Familiarity with scripting languages (such as Python, PowerShell, or Bash) will be crucial for automating repetitive tasks and enhancing threat hunting workflows. Automation can significantly increase the efficiency of data collection and analysis.

2.2 Analytical Skills

Data Analysis and Visualization: Future threat hunters must be adept at analyzing large datasets to identify patterns, trends, and anomalies. Proficiency in data visualization tools can help them present findings in a clear and actionable manner.

Threat Intelligence Analysis: Understanding how to interpret and leverage threat intelligence will be vital. Threat hunters should be skilled in assessing the relevance and credibility of threat intelligence sources and integrating this information into their hunting strategies.

Critical Thinking and Problem Solving: Threat hunters must be able to approach complex problems methodically, identifying the root causes of incidents and developing effective strategies to address them. Strong analytical thinking skills will be key in formulating hypotheses and validating findings.

2.3 Soft Skills

Effective Communication: The ability to communicate complex technical concepts to non-technical stakeholders is essential. Future threat hunters must be capable of articulating the significance of their findings and recommendations in a way that resonates with diverse audiences, including executive leadership.

Collaboration and Teamwork: Given the interconnected nature of cybersecurity, threat hunters will need to work closely with various teams within the organization. Strong interpersonal skills and the ability to collaborate effectively will enhance their impact.

Adaptability and Resilience: The cybersecurity landscape is constantly changing, and threat hunters must be adaptable to new technologies, threats, and methodologies. Resilience in the face of setbacks will also be crucial for maintaining a proactive approach to threat hunting.

3. Specialized Knowledge Areas

As cyber threats continue to evolve, threat hunters will benefit from developing specialized knowledge in specific areas:

3.1 Understanding Emerging Threats

Ransomware Tactics: Given the rise of ransomware attacks, threat hunters should familiarize themselves with the tactics employed by ransomware actors, including social engineering techniques and exploit kits.

Internet of Things (IoT) Security: As the IoT landscape expands, understanding the unique security challenges associated with IoT devices will become increasingly important for threat hunters.

Cloud Security: Knowledge of cloud security principles and architectures will be essential as organizations migrate to cloud environments. Threat hunters must understand how to detect and respond to threats in cloud-based infrastructures.

3.2 Knowledge of Regulations and Compliance

Legal and Compliance Frameworks: Threat hunters should be aware of relevant legal and regulatory frameworks, such as GDPR, HIPAA, and PCI-DSS, as these regulations often dictate how organizations must handle security incidents and data breaches.

Ethical Considerations: A solid understanding of the ethical implications of threat hunting, including privacy concerns and responsible data handling, will be critical in ensuring that threat hunters operate within legal boundaries while conducting their activities.

4. Continuous Learning and Professional Development

To keep pace with the rapidly evolving cybersecurity landscape, future threat hunters must prioritize continuous learning and professional development:

4.1 Certifications and Training Programs

Cybersecurity Certifications: Earning industry-recognized certifications, such as Certified Information Systems Security Professional (CISSP), Certified Ethical Hacker (CEH), or GIAC Cyber Threat Intelligence (GCTI), can enhance a threat hunter's credibility and expertise.

Ongoing Training: Participating in training programs, workshops, and online courses focused on emerging technologies, threat hunting methodologies, and soft skills development will help threat hunters stay current with the latest trends and best practices.

4.2 Engaging with the Community

Networking and Collaboration: Threat hunters should engage with the cybersecurity community through forums, conferences, and social media platforms. Networking with peers can provide valuable insights and foster collaboration.

Sharing Knowledge: Contributing to open-source projects, writing articles, or presenting at conferences can help threat hunters share their knowledge and learn from others, further enhancing their skills and expertise.

The future of threat hunting will demand a diverse skill set that encompasses technical proficiency, analytical acumen, and interpersonal abilities. As cyber threats continue to evolve, threat hunters must adapt and refine their skills to remain effective in identifying and mitigating risks. By prioritizing continuous learning, specialized knowledge development, and collaboration, future threat hunters will be well-equipped to navigate the complexities of the cybersecurity landscape. Embracing these skills will not only enhance their individual capabilities but also contribute to the resilience and security of the organizations they serve. In a world where the threat landscape is ever-changing, the ability to adapt and evolve will define the success of future threat hunters.

In **The Threat Landscape: Navigating Cyber Threat Hunting**, *Sergey Sokolovea* provides a comprehensive guide to the proactive practice of threat hunting in an increasingly complex and hostile digital environment. This book equips cybersecurity professionals, IT teams, and newcomers alike with the essential knowledge and skills needed to anticipate, detect, and respond to cyber threats before they escalate into significant incidents.

Starting with foundational concepts, the book explores the modern threat landscape, identifying key threat types, adversaries, and their evolving tactics. It outlines the critical components of building an effective threat hunting program, emphasizing the importance of integrating threat intelligence and leveraging the right tools and technologies.

Readers will learn the step-by-step processes of hypothesis-driven hunting, data collection, and investigative techniques, as well as advanced methodologies like behavioral analysis, deception tactics, and incident response integration. The author emphasizes the importance of continuous improvement, ethical considerations, and the future of threat hunting, ensuring readers are well-prepared to navigate the ever-evolving cyber threat landscape.

With practical examples, case studies, and actionable strategies, The Threat Landscape is not just a manual for today's challenges but a forward-looking resource that encourages resilience and adaptability in the face of emerging threats. Whether you are a seasoned professional seeking to refine your skills or a newcomer eager to make an impact, this book will empower you to become a more effective threat hunter, contributing to the ongoing battle for cybersecurity.

www.ingramcontent.com/pod-product-compliance
Lightning Source LLC
Chambersburg PA
CBHW062105220526
45471CB00010B/3612